D1571859

DATE DUE

ALCHEMY IN A GLASS

The Essential Guide to Handcrafted Cocktails

GREG SEIDER

PHOTOGRAPHS BY NOAH FECKS

FOREWORD BY JIM MEEHAN

RIZZOLI
NEW YORK

CONTENTS

FOREWORD

Both Greg Seider and I have worked in many roles in the bar business for the better part of two decades, operate cocktail bars across a park from one another in New York City's East Village, and now share the distinction of being cocktail book authors. Like opening a bar in a neighborhood filled with them, writing a cocktail book poses its own ontological dilemma: What do you have to add to the extensive existing body of work going all the way to back to Jerry Thomas's seminal 1862 guide?

When Seider said he was working on a book, I told him what I tell every talented bartender who says they want to open their own bar: "Are you sure you want to do this?" Don't get me wrong; after traveling the world to visit distilleries, present at and attend bar shows, and guest bartending at some of the world's most celebrated speaks, I can say without a shred of a doubt that the author of this book has created some of the most nuanced cocktails I've ever had the privilege of imbibing.

But the skills required to rise to the top of the New York City cocktail scene don't prepare you for the humbling process of laying your life's work down on paper for customers who will have to invest a bit of time and money— not to mention roll up their own sleeves—to see if you put your pen where your palate is. For anyone second-guessing the author's instructions, I heartily implore you to reconsider.

Before you is one of the most personal accounts of making drinks that's ever been published. I've always wondered what makes Seider's drinks stand out, and after reading his book, it's clear that he's never let history—or propriety for that matter— get in the way of a good story, or the conventional mixing customs cloud his unique vision for cocktail creation and service.

Bawdy barroom recollections such as the story behind Say Hello to My Little Friend, unique and beguilingly simple techniques such as adding the effervescent ingredient to your shaker and pouring instead of topping, and a dissertation on how to use spices in cocktails, inspired by the way master chef Eric Ripert does in his food, are just a few of the highlights of this book, which painstakingly explains not only how to make drinks, but what role each ingredient has in the complex equation he calls alchemy.

In the tradition of the original alchemists, Seider's cocktails achieve a flavor profile that is more complex than the sum of their parts. If I could give this book its subtitle, I'd call it "Straight no Chaser," as Seider has all but captured his unique charm as a bartender in the beautifully photographed narrative as an author. Cheers to that sir.

- JIM MEEHAN

INTRODUCTION

HOW SEIDER BECAME SEIDER

I made my first cocktail at the ripe old age of ten. My *oma* (grandmother) used to visit our family in Rhode Island during the summer, cooking up a storm while nurturing her peculiar obsession with Burgundy wine, particularly that of the jug variety. Following in the family fondness for the work of E & J Gallo, I developed a personal taste for Bartles & Jaymes wine coolers at a young age. My father would often give me a sip of his after I helped him cut the grass. (If he wasn't looking, I could finish a whole bottle.) One memorable summer day, I snuck out to the garage with a glass of ice, poured myself a bit of wine, and topped it with ginger ale and a slice of orange. Thus my journey into the world of cocktail creation ostensibly began, and I haven't looked back.

For as long as I can remember, I've been a supertaster. As a kid, my body was riddled with allergies, and I often could barely breathe through my nose, a situation that had the effect of helping me to over-develop my sense of taste to compensate. My oversensitive palate has proven to be the key element that guides my creativity, and it has also made me extremely discerning about flavor and balance in everything I taste. Luckily for me, I was raised on food made from a cornucopia of fresh ingredients. My parents created a Garden of Eden of sorts in the backyard of the house I grew up in. The top yard was filled with herbs, fresh berries, rhubarb, and a trellis with two varieties of grapes. The lower yard had apple and peach trees, and the main garden had just about every other fruit or vegetable imaginable, or so it seemed to me as a child. In addition, the town I grew up in was on the water, so fresh mussels, clams, and fish were always at our fingertips. So you could say I was a spoiled child, having been given access to such a wide variety of fresh flavors—the cornerstone of gustatory greatness—right out of the gate. These two conditions of my childhood, along with my precocious enthusiasm for mixing drinks, combined to create an enduring passion to understand and manipulate the way different ingredients interact to produce an overall flavor, which has led me to create this book.

HOW MING TSAI AND THE FOOD NETWORK SAVED MY LIFE

In 2001, after getting my feet wet at '90s hotspots Asia de Cuba and Lot 61, I moved to L.A., where due to the not-so-unfamiliar circumstances of being a man in his twenties with too much time on his hands, I quickly ran out of money. For the first time since I left for college, I had to move back in with my parents. It was the dead of winter, and as I was trying to figure out a way to get back to New York, a certain degree of desperation set in. To keep my sanity, I began to watch the Food Network obsessively, especially Ming Tsai's Asian cooking show, *East Meets West*. The exotic ingredients and the bright, layered flavors of his recipes left me bright-eyed and bushy-tailed, and inspired me to get back into action. I began experimenting with my own combinations of flavors, using techniques and ingredients I learned from Ming, Alton Brown, Mario Batali, and the rest of the Food Network lineup. I managed to escape Rhode Island (and my TV addiction) and got my chops back working behind the bar at Town, a restaurant in the Chambers Hotel in Manhattan.

Everything came together when I moved on to the bar at Mercer Kitchen in the early 2000s. Jean-Georges Vongerichten's food (and especially his use of Asian flavors) really resonated with me and in turn gave me inspiration for creating drinks. I became fast friends with the pastry chef, Karen Hatfield, and, using her fruit purees and spiced syrups, I began to experiment. I started making trips down to Chinatown, and was introduced to a whole new crop of ingredients with unusual, exquisite tastes that I had never considered using in drinks

before. Lemongrass, calamansi, yuzu, shiso, and Thai basil were my way into the up-and-coming, culinary-inspired cocktail scene and helped me develop my signature style of layering flavors in a drink. I developed personalized "off-menu" drinks for people based on their tastes and moods, often surprising them with a spice or fruit or herb. Once I had a large enough clientele, I was able to leave the Mercer and, with my partner Hamid, open Summit Bar and then Prima restaurant, where I was finally able to put some of these recipes down on paper (menus) and had the freedom to continue to experiment to my heart's content.

4-STAR INGREDIENTS= 4-STAR COCKTAILS

In 2011, I had the extraordinary pleasure to create the cocktail program for the lounge at Le Bernardin. Working with Chef Eric Ripert, Soa Davies, and sommelier Aldo Sohm raised my creative process to new levels. I learned the importance of sourcing not just unusual ingredients but ones of the highest quality. I learned what freshness really tastes like. (I also learned that, damn, do I love me some Scottish langoustine.) Many of the individual special ingredients we worked with—peach blossom rooibos tea, smoked cinnamon—lent multiple dimensions to a dish or a drink, creating complex layers of flavors. The greatest lesson I learned from Chef Ripert is that you can achieve complexity in your food or cocktail simply by sourcing great ingredients. He taught me the magic of sourcing, and I taught him about the deliciousness of Japanese whiskey. (Let's just call it even.)

GRAPEFRUIT SAFFRON KAFFIR LIME SARSAPARILLA

At Le Bernardin, I was challenged to create drinks that would have as many dimensions as the food and wine. It was the ultimate game of Jenga: If I didn't use just the right components in precise amounts, it could throw off the entire balance of a great drink-in-the-making. Sometimes I made a dozen versions of a cocktail, with miniscule adjustments each time, before it got the green light by Chef and the team. This rite of passage resulted in a higher knowledge of how to balance and elevate flavors in the beginning, middle, and finishing stages of the drink, and gave me the inspiration for the cocktail layering principle I use in this book.

INSPIRATION:
THE ESSENCE OF CREATING A GREAT DRINK

A cocktail, in my mind, is not just a recipe. It's an opportunity to tell a story, to stir up memories, feelings, and sensations. These stories, like the gardens of my childhood home, help anchor me and spark the crucial "aha!" moment of inspiration fueled by ingredients, environment, and the circumstances in which I'm mixing drinks. My instincts for flavors guide me through an alchemic process of layering and combining that culminates in capturing a feeling of nostalgia and, more important, a kick-ass drink.

The name of a drink helps anchor me in a moment or image of inspiration, and sparks that necessary but sometimes elusive "aha-ness." At Summit, I couldn't put a drink on the menu unless the name felt as alluring as the combination of ingredients. Ground to Glass, The Guv'nor, Charmane Star, Breaking the Law—all of these drinks achieved cult status thanks in part to their memorable names, but it was also the names that connected me to the stories behind them. Often I'll start with a story, or a memory, or an idea, and think of a catchy title for it. Then my instincts about flavor and combining take over, with the inspiration driving the alchemic process that hopefully culminates in the aforementioned kick-ass drink.

> Harness the good energy, block out the bad. Harness. Energy. Block. Bad. It's like a carousel. You put the quarter in, you get on the horse, it goes up and down and around. Circular, circle. Feel it. Go with the flow.
>
> —KEVIN NEALON AS GARY POTTER IN *HAPPY GILMORE*

THERE IS COMPLEXITY IN SIMPLICITY

I create unique flavors in my drinks by using sensual and evocative ingredients, like toasted cardamom, peach blossom rooibos, and smoked cinnamon, along with my beloved shiso, lemongrass, and yuzu from my Chinatown days. But a great drink must have a blueprint, a behind-the-scenes understanding of the ingredients and how they balance themselves along different parts of the palate. Classic cocktails, in all their historic glory, lay a foundation for a simple but effective idea: The whole is greater than the sum of its parts. Advancing this concept for a modern age, the Alchemist approach goes further in understanding how different components like sweet, spice, bitters, and aromatic work in a drink, and how we can elevate these elements to take any drink, old or new, to soaring new heights.

CLASSICS + INSPIRATION = ELEVATION

There are plenty of cocktail menus whose drinks sound great on paper. But throwing together exotic and unusual ingredients is only the first step. Understanding how ingredients go together (and in what proportions) is what allows them to shine in a glass, either in harmonious balance or as an experience of contrasts. A knowledge of the classics is key, as is looking at each drink as a series of layers, which is why in this book, I've broken my each of my original recipes down into three elements: Foundation, Dimension, and Finish.

When you make any drink—whether it be a tried-and-true Manhattan or one of my yuzu-gin-shiso concoctions—you want to ask yourself the same questions: Can you taste every ingredient? When and where on the palate do you taste each one? Are they separate but complementary, or do they combine to create a wholly new flavor? These questions are the cornerstones of this book. *Alchemy in a Glass* is an initiation into the mysterious equation of flavors, techniques, storytelling, and inspiration that goes into every cocktail, and will guide you through the magic transformation from collection of ingredients to masterful drink.

> Learn the rules so you know how to break them properly.
>
> —DALAI LAMA

SEIDER AND THE ART OF FLAVORCYCLE MAINTENANCE

THE MECHANICS OF BUILDING KICK-ASS ALCHEMIST COCKTAILS ARE PRETTY SIMPLE. Every drink is made from the same four sequential layers: foundation, dimension, finish, and the X-factor. The magic, however, is in the details. The chart on page 16 describes how within each layer, flavors, textures, and ingredients can be combined to do their work in a drink. The alchemy depends upon how different combinations of foundations, dimensions, and finishes—combined with nostalgia, emotion, and inspiration—result in distinctive, harmonious blends that play out over the course of a drink.

Whenever possible, use fresh and homemade ingredients in your drinks. There are recipes for many of the components of these drinks (such as mixes, infusions, tinctures, bitters, purees, and garnishes) in the back of this book. Fresh, homemade ingredients will not only taste better, they will also give you more control over the precise flavor balance in the drink because you'll know exactly what is going into it. Use non-homemade flavored spirits, cordials, and other prepackaged ingredients at your own risk.*

DON'T BECOME A MEMBER OF M.A.A.
(MARASCHINO ADDICTS ANONYMOUS)

The **foundation** is achieved by using a correct proportion of spirit, sweet, and sour. You cannot progress to adding additional flavors to a drink until you perfect this fundamental balance. You are trying to blend these three different elements to create a process along the palate, during which you should be able to detect specific characteristics of each element at different points. The spirit should present first; you should be able to taste its distinct character without being overwhelmed by alcohol.

The sweet is there to highlight the middle of the palate, but be aware that too much sweet will make the drink feel flat and will coat your mouth. Sour enables a clean, dry finish, but can take over the drink with a tart or bitter taste. You know you have achieved a good balance among these three elements when you get an equal sense of each, before you add anything else.

This harmony can be created with pretty much any spirit, but it's much easier to do with shaken drinks than with stirred ones.

{ ALCHEMIST FOOLPROOF, }
{ WHEN-IN-DOUBT FORMULA FOR SHAKEN DRINKS }

This is the basic formula I use to come up with proportions for any shaken drink, short or tall. You can substitute any type of spirit or sweet as long as the sweet is in close proximity of sweetness to agave mix or simple syrup (which both have one-to-one ratios of water and sweetener). Citrus usually means fresh lime, lemon, or grapefruit juice.

SHORT	2 ounces spirit	+ 1 ounce citrus	+ ¾ ounce sweet	
GIN GIMLET	2 ounces gin	1 ounce lime juice	¾ ounce agave mix	
DAIQUIRI	2 ounces rum	1 ounce lime juice	¾ ounce agave mix	
TALL	2 ounces spirit	+ ¾ ounce citrus	+ ¾ ounce sweet	+ 1 ounce soda
TOM COLLINS	2 ounces gin	¾ ounce lemon juice	¾ ounce agave mix	1 ounce club soda
BREAKING THE LAW	2 ounces spirit (1 ounce mezcal + 1 ounce Dimmi)	¾ ounce lime juice	¾ ounce chipotle chile agave mix	1 ounce club soda

With stirred drinks, coming up with a foundation from scratch is harder, since they can include cordials and liqueurs, which are themselves complex blends of spirit, sweet, herbal, and/or sour.

The **dimension** of a drink is what gives it flicker and pop. The dimension ignites the palate through the four basic tastes (sweet, salty, bitter, sour) by using more complex elements such as herbs, fruits, spices, smoke, teas, tinctures, and ingredients with piquant, exotic, or garden qualities. A beautifully balanced drink can be achieved with six or seven components, but unless you are really a master Alchemist, choose only one ingredient from within each category. For instance, you can mix basil (herb) and cinnamon (spice), but not basil and another herb. Two or more ingredients from the same category can easily muddy the flavor balance, and will prevent you from being able to taste all the ingredients in harmony. (The exception to this are bitters and tinctures, which work to bind ingredients and highlight specific flavor components.) Yes, adding that innocent sprig of rosemary might just blow the whole drink!

The **finish** has different, equally important aspects: mouthfeel, texture, and aromatic quality. Whether a drink is shaken or stirred will affect the mouthfeel and texture, as shaking gives it aeration and froth while stirring results in a viscous mouthfeel. Also, adding egg white or effervescent components and salting or powdering glass rims adds texture and thus another layer to the overall experience of your drink. **Aromatics** are thought to be responsible for the majority of flavor you perceive. Citrus zest, herbs, ground spices, and atomized spirits are some of the main aromatic options you have to manipulate the finish of your drink, so that it's fresh, bright, exotic, or smoky, respectively.

A drink's **X-factor** is that mystical, invisible component. It is the emotional connection evoked by the drink in which the name, a story, or a moment of inspiration drives the specific combination of ingredients inside the glass. Epic adventures, people loved and lost, and childhood memories can all come through in the journey of each drink. When you develop a cocktail, you need to bring your heart and mind into the process as well as your senses of taste and smell. And don't forget to say a little prayer to the bar gods when you shake it up for the first time . . .

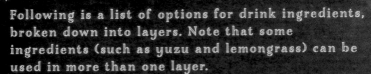

Following is a list of options for drink ingredients, broken down into layers. Note that some ingredients (such as yuzu and lemongrass) can be used in more than one layer.

FOUNDATION

The foundation is achieved by using a correct proportion of spirit, sweet, and sour.

. . . .

SPIRIT: Vodka, gin, rum, Bourbon, rye, tequila, mezcal, Scotch . . .

SOUR: Lemon juice, lime juice, grapefruit juice, yuzu juice, kumquat juice, dry wine (such as Sauvignon Blanc)

SWEET: Agave mixes, simple syrup, honey, cordials, liqueurs

DIMENSION

The dimension of a drink is what gives it flicker and pop.

. . . .

HERBS: All types of mint, basil, rosemary, thyme, lemon verbena, lemon thyme, sage, lavender, shiso

FRUIT (WHOLE, PUREED, JUICE, OR NECTAR): All types of berries, Morello cherry, blood orange, calamansi, peach, pear

SAVORY/GARDEN: Cucumber, tomato, carrot, red pepper

SPICE (GROUND, OR INFUSED WHOLE INTO SPIRITS OR AGAVE MIXES): Vietnamese cinnamon, cardamom, black peppercorn, pink peppercorn, Szechuan peppercorn, clove, ginger, nutmeg, Chinese five-spice, allspice, fennel, star anise

PIQUANT: Whole or dried chiles such as jalapeño or serrano, horseradish, wasabi

SMOKE: Lapsang Souchong tea, chipotle chiles, Scotch

EXOTICS: Yuzu, kaffir lime leaves, lemongrass

TEAS: Rooibos, honey bush, green, Moroccan mint, peach, hibiscus

BITTERS: orange, angostura, kaffir lime, grapefruit, rhubarb, peach

TINCTURES: Spiced cranberry, lemongrass peppercorn, kaffir lime, sarsaparilla, saffron, smoked cinnamon, rooibos

FINISH

The finish has different, equally important aspects: mouthfeel, texture, and aromatic quality.

....

HERBS: Smacked mint leaf, lemon thyme

CITRUS PEELS OR ZEST: Lemon, lime, grapefruit, orange

ATOMIZED TINCTURE OR SPIRIT: Mist of aromatic spirit such as smoky Scotch or absinthe

GROUND SPICES: Cardamom, nutmeg, clove

TEXTURE: Flavored salts, egg white

EFFERVESCENCE: Sparkling wine, club soda, carbonated beverage, beer

THE X-FACTOR

A drink's X-factor is that mystical, invisible component, the emotional connection evoked by the drink.

....

EXPERIENCE: Travels, memories of loved ones, childhood experiences

CULTURE: Songs, books, movies, stories

INSPIRATION: From anywhere!

SPIRIT

Sweet

Mixing
Glass

Julep
Strainer

Bitters

Aromatic

Jigger

CLASSICS

OLD FASHIONED

With its breezy notes of American individualism, the Old Fashioned (sometimes referred to as "the Original") is sophisticated in its simplicity, but complex in the wild interpretations it has inspired through the annals of cocktail history. The Old Fashioned is often considered the original cocktail, an American-born invention defined by its combination of spirit, sugar, and bitters stirred with a handsome lump of ice, then strained. Many trace this drink's birth to the Pendennis Club in late-nineteenth-century Louisville, made either by or in honor of a one Col. James E. Pepper, a patriarch of Kentucky Bourbon. Then Prohibition arrived, and, like many other first-wave cocktails, the original Old Fashioned recipe was lost and the drink mutated into many bastard forms until it was revived again by a new culture of cocktail purists.

SEIDER'S FORMULA

SPIRIT	2 ounces Knob Creek rye
BITTERS	2 dashes orange bitters
BITTERS	2 dashes Angostura bitters
SWEET	¼ ounce agave mix (page 136)

METHOD

Stir all the ingredients with ice in a mixing glass. Strain and pour over fresh ice.

GLASS	Rocks
GARNISH	Orange peel
NOTABLE SUBSTITUTIONS	Rittenhouse rye, Jefferson's Reserve 15-year Bourbon, Buffalo Trace Bourbon, Knob Creek Single Barrel Reserve

ALCHEMIST NOTE

Although one of the more popular spirits in America before Prohibition, straight rye was hard to come by during much of the twentieth century. The spirit has experienced a resurgence in recent years, and Knob Creek rye in particular is assertive enough to hold its own in a cocktail. Its hints of cinnamon, pepper, and wood provide a subtle undertone when mixed into a drink. Orange bitters add a brightness that results in a bold yet layered take on a classic.

MARTINI

The origins of the Martini are still hotly debated. Some trace its ancestry to a drink called the Martinez, served to a gold miner on his way to Martinez, California, by the famed bartender "Professor" Jerry Thomas at the Occidental Hotel in San Francisco in the 1860s. This drink was a peculiar mix of one dash of Boker's bitters, two dashes of Maraschino liqueur, one pony of Old Tom gin, and a wine glass of vermouth. Others claim it originated in the town of Martinez itself, where, in 1870, bartender Julio Richelieu made a concoction of gin and vermouth with a curious surprise dropped in: an olive. New Yorkers often claim it was invented by Martini di Arma di Taggia at the Knickerbocker Hotel for famed billionaire John D. Rockefeller. In a rarer account, the name "martini" originated in the British army in the late 1800s, describing carriers of the Martini-Henry rifle, and came to refer to drinkers of a concoction with a similar "strong kick." Speculation aside, the Martini has become an international symbol of cool, regardless of whether one prefers the Rat Pack or James Bond, shaken or stirred, gin or vodka, dry or wet. But purists insist the only acceptable recipe uses gin and dry vermouth, which is then stirred, strained, and garnished with an olive or lemon peel, depending upon which side of history your heart lies.

ALCHEMIST NOTE

Good-quality vermouth is the key to a great Martini. The botanicals in Dolin dry complement the blend of herbs and aromatics from my choice gin, No. 3, a modern twist on the traditional spirit with a proprietary blend of juniper, grapefruit, Seville orange, angelica root, coriander, and cardamom, elevating it above the normal London dry gin.

SEIDER'S FORMULA

SPIRIT	2½ ounces No. 3 London Dry gin (or Russian Standard vodka)
SWEET/FLORAL	½ ounce Dolin dry vermouth

METHOD

Stir all the ingredients with ice in a mixing glass. Strain and serve up.

GLASS	Martini or coupe
GARNISH	Olive skewer
NOTABLE SUBSTITUTIONS	Beefeater, Bombay Sapphire East (London dry gin); Plymouth, Spring 44, Ford's, Brooklyn (New American/ New Western gin)

ALCHEMIST NOTE

As in a Martini, the vermouth you select will make or break your Manhattan. My choice of vermouth, Dolin, is fresh, restrained, and elegant without the cloying sweetness found in many other vermouths. Combine this with the dry spice of a solid rye whiskey and the singular zing of orange bitters, and, like magic, you've got a smooth cocktail that is more than the sum of its parts.

MANHATTAN

According to cocktail lore, the Manhattan was brought into this world in New York City in the mid-1870s at a banquet for Lady Randolph Churchill. This legend has been summarily dismissed by the venerable cocktail expert David Wondrich, given that Lady Randolph was living in London at the time, about to give birth to her baby, Winston. A more likely history comes from an account by a New York bartender named William F. Mulhall. He wrote "the Manhattan Cocktail was invented by a man named Black, who kept a place ten doors below Houston Street on Broadway in the 1860s." The Manhattan was one of the first drinks to utilize vermouth as a modifier (which smoothes the harshness of a spirit without taking over the flavor), predating other famed vermouth-flecked cocktails such as the Martini. Although it is acceptable to use Bourbon, the original recipe calls for straight rye whiskey (a staple of nineteenth-century spirits), aromatic bitters, and sweet vermouth.

SEIDER'S FORMULA

SPIRIT	2 ounces Rittenhouse rye
SWEET	1 ounce Dolin sweet vermouth
BITTERS	2 dashes orange bitters
BITTERS	2 dashes Angostura bitters

METHOD

Stir all the ingredients with ice in a mixing glass. Strain and serve up.

GLASS	Martini or coupe
GARNISH	Bourbon-soaked cherry (page 145)
NOTABLE SUBSTITUTIONS	Cocchi Vermouth di Torino (vermouth); Knob Creek rye, Eagle Rare 10-year-old Bourbon (rye/Bourbon)

DAIQUIRI

In his journals, Leonardo da Vinci wrote that "Simplicity is the ultimate sophistication." What could be more simple than rum, lime juice, and sugar? In 1905, an American mining engineer working in the town of Daiquiri on the southeast coast of Cuba wrote about this delicious concoction, but considering the abundance of sugarcane and rum in the region, a version of the Daiquiri was likely consumed in the Caribbean long before this first recorded account. The new cocktail remained a purely Cuban phenomenon until 1909, when a U.S. navy medical officer discovered it and introduced the tropical drink at the Army and Navy Club in Washington, D.C. From there, it became a wildly popular and oft romanticized concoction, with the likes of F. Scott Fitzgerald and Ernest Hemingway touting its magnificence. Hemingway lived in Cuba during the 1930s and was a regular at the El Floridita bar in Havana. There, he was introduced to a variation on the original recipe that came to be known as the Hemingway Daiquiri by bartender Constante Ribalaigua (also creator of the Floridita, a cousin to the Hemingway Daiquiri), which left out the sugar and added a dash of grapefruit juice and Maraschino liqueur. But the original recipe is an ode to simplicity itself, and many think the merit of a great barman depends upon his skill in carefully creating a perfect balance between the holy trinity of ingredients, as one cannot bluff when dealing with such simple elegance.

ALCHEMIST NOTE

Banks Island Rum, my first choice for a Daiquiri, has a dry, funky, sugarcane flavor, which brings a unique quality to this drink. It has a silky mouthfeel and an angular, dry sugarcane flavor, which makes for an ideal mixing rum. Substituting agave mix for sugar leads to a silkier finish that balances well with the tartness of the lime juice.

SEIDER'S FORMULA

SPIRIT	2 ounces Banks Island rum
SOUR	1 ounce fresh lime juice
SWEET	¾ ounce agave mix (page 136)

METHOD

Shake all the ingredients with ice in a shaker tin. Double strain and serve up or pour over fresh ice.

GLASS	Coupe or rocks
GARNISH	Lime zest
NOTABLE SUBSTITUTIONS	Flor de Caña 4-year-old Extra Dry White, Cana Brava

ALCHEMIST NOTE

My take on this classic recipe finds a harmonious balance between tart and sweet, which, in turn, allows the distinct flavors of the blue agave plant to shine through the tequila. Substituting for the more standard triple sec or Cointreau, agave mix and Regan's orange bitters allow for an auspicious finish without a syrupy mouthfeel. Please, ladies and gentlemen, treat Ms. Margarita right. Leave out the triple sec!

MARGARITA

Like many historic cocktails, the story behind the Margarita is murky. As one popular tale goes, while visiting a bar in Rosarito Beach, Mexico, a Ziegfeld girl named Marjorie King professed an allergy to all alcohol save for tequila and asked the bartender, Danny Herrera, to make her a drink. He summarily poured tequila over shaved ice, added lemon and triple sec, and served up his new creation. Needing a name for it, he translated *Marjorie* to the Spanish equivalent, *Margarita*. Much less poetic (though more likely) origins date back to a nineteenth-century standard, the Gin Daisy. This evolved into the Tequila Daisy, a drink popular with soldiers during World War II, that combined tequila, citrus juice, and grenadine.

SEIDER'S FORMULA

SPIRIT	2 ounces Cabeza blanco tequila
SOUR	1 ounce fresh lime juice
SWEET	¾ ounce agave mix (page 136)
BITTERS	2 dashes Regan's orange bitters

METHOD

Shake all the ingredients in a shaker tin. Double strain and pour over fresh ice.

GLASS	Rocks
GARNISH	Lime zest
NOTABLE SUBSTITUTIONS	El Tesoro Platinum, Olmeca Altos plata

SIDECAR

With a history spanning over a century, the Sidecar is the most venerable of brandy cocktails. The most romantic story of its origin comes from Paris sometime after World War I, which has the drink named for the motorcycle sidecar of an American captain who would ride to his favorite watering hole, a little-known place called Harry's Bar. As the story goes, one infamous evening there was a chill in the air, and the captain requested a pre-dinner nip to warm him up. Brandy was the obvious choice, but serving an after-dinner drink before a meal was considered a *faux pas*. But necessity is the mother of invention, and the barman created a cocktail more fitting to the hour: a curious blend of brandy, orange curaçao, and lemon juice. Another more likely origin, however, is that the Sidecar (like the Margarita) comes from the family of pre-Prohibition cocktails known as Daisies. Nevertheless, a chilly, enchanted night in Paris suits this cocktail just fine.

SEIDER'S FORMULA

SPIRIT	2 ounces Soberano brandy
SWEET	¾ ounce agave mix (page 136)
SOUR	¾ ounce fresh lime juice
BITTERS	2 dashes orange bitters

METHOD

Shake all the ingredients with ice in a shaker tin. Double strain and serve up.

GLASS	Coupe
GARNISH	Lime zest
NOTABLE SUBSTITUTIONS	Pierre Ferrand Ambre, Martell VS

ALCHEMIST NOTE

Soberano brandy is produced from Airén grapes from the La Mancha region of Spain. Its slight nuttiness and cinnamon tones give it a roundness that pairs well in a cocktail, without the harshness of most entry-level Cognacs. The lime zest adds an aromatic flavor of sharp citrus, creating a more complex finish on the palete.

JACK ROSE

Featured in Hemingway's *The Sun Also Rises*, the Jack Rose, a variation on the Sidecar, most likely originated in Jersey City at Gene Sullivan's Café, near the birthplace of its core ingredient, apple brandy, otherwise known as applejack, the state spirit of New Jersey. According to David Wondrich's history *Imbibe!*, the inventor of the drink was announced in the *Police Gazette* in 1905 as "Frank J. May, better known as Jack Rose." A more colorful version of the Jack Rose's birth claims that an infamous gambler and New York City gangster, Jacob Rosenzweig, had the cocktail named after him, having been nicknamed by those who knew him as "Bald Jack Rose." Legends aside, this peculiar apple-flavored concoction remains a staple in the ledgers of bar history.

SEIDER'S FORMULA

SPIRIT	2 ounces Château du Breuil or VSOP Calvados
SOUR/CITRUS	¾ ounce fresh lemon juice
SWEET	¾ ounce homemade grenadine syrup (page 138)
BITTERS	2 dashes orange bitters

METHOD

Shake all the ingredients with ice in a shaker tin. Double strain and serve up.

GLASS	Coupe
GARNISH	Orange zest
NOTABLE SUBSTITUTIONS	Menorval, Clear Creek barrel-aged brandy, Boulard VSOP Pays d'Auge Calvados

NEGRONI

On what one would like to think was a sweltering summer day in Italy in 1919, a nobleman by the name of Count Camillo Negroni asked his local bartender for his usual: Campari, sweet vermouth, and soda. As the story goes, just as the barman was about to make the drink, the count asked him to jazz up the usual concoction. The bartender obliged by adding a spot of gin, and thus the Negroni was born. Although simple on paper, the intricacy of preparing the perfect Negroni is a balancing act verging on art form. Does harmony exist in equal parts gin, sweet vermouth, and Campari? Or will a dash more gin make it that much jazzier? This is where a simple drink becomes an exploration of taste—and where the devil is indeed in the details of proportion.

SEIDER'S FORMULA

SPIRIT	1½ ounces No. 3 London Dry gin
SPIRIT/SWEET	¾ ounce Aperol
SWEET	¾ ounce Dolin sweet vermouth
BITTERS	2 dashes Regan's orange bitters

METHOD

Shake all the ingredients with ice in a shaker tin. Double strain and pour over fresh ice.

GLASS	Rocks
GARNISH	Orange zest
NOTABLE SUBSTITUTIONS	Plymouth, Ford's, Bombay Sapphire East

ALCHEMIST NOTE

The proportions of this create a more palatable Negroni than what is commonly used. Equal gin, sweet vermouth, a Campari is very bitter; use of Aperol provides the right amount of bi and its rhubarb and ora notes marry nicely wit orange bitters, the aro botanicals, and suavity sweet vermouth.

ALCHEMIST NOTE
The Boulevardier is a Bourbon lover's Negroni, so the core spirit should shine through. Substituting the bitterness of Campari with the mellow tinge of Aperol (as in my Negroni) allows the nuances of Kentucky's best to come out. Adding a complex vermouth with a dash of citrus bitters gives this somewhat intimidating classic a dose of modernity.

BOULEVARDIER

A distant and nearly forgotten cousin of the Negroni (or a bastard stepchild of the Manhattan, depending on how you see it), the Boulevardier, created by Harry McElhone, came into existence in 1927 at Harry's Bar in Paris. The recipe appeared in his extraordinary book, *Barflies and Cocktails*, and the drink was apparently a favorite of Erskine Gwynne, a socialite and writer (and nephew of Alfred Vanderbilt) who edited a magazine by the name of—you guessed it—*The Boulevardier*. With two parts rye or Bourbon, one part Campari, and one part sweet vermouth, the cocktail is yet another example of how harmony can be found within a bevy of ingredients.

SEIDER'S FORMULA

SPIRIT	1½ ounces Jefferson Reserve Bourbon
SWEET	¾ ounce Dolin sweet vermouth
BITTER/SWEET	¾ ounce Aperol
BITTERS	2 dashes orange bitters

METHOD

Shake all the ingredients with ice in a shaker tin. Double strain and pour over fresh ice.

GLASS	Rocks
GARNISH	Orange zest
NOTABLE SUBSTITUTIONS	Eagle Rare 10-year-old Bourbon, Basil Hayden's Bourbon, Elijah Craig 12-year-old Bourbon, Knob Creek rye

SAZERAC

In the annals of classic cocktails, there are few drinks that have the intricacy of preparation or the boldness of flavor as the Sazerac. Known as a quintessential New Orleans cocktail (it was named the official cocktail of the city of New Orleans by the state legislature in 2008), the Sazerac was invented in the nineteenth century by a Creole apothecary by the name of Antoine Amadie Peychaud (also inventor of the eponymous bitters), who named it for his favorite French brandy, Sazerac de Forge et Fils. In 1870, the recipe was altered when American rye whiskey was substituted for Cognac, and a dash of absinthe was added by bartender Leon Lamothe, who is now regarded as the Father of the Sazerac.

SEIDER'S FORMULA

SPIRIT	Absinthe mist
SPIRIT	2 ounces Knob Creek rye
SWEET	¼ ounce fennel-infused agave mix (page 137)
BITTERS	2 dashes orange bitters
BITTERS	2 dashes Peychaud's bitters

METHOD

Using an atomizer, spray absinthe into a chilled glass. Stir the remaining ingredients with ice in a mixing glass. Strain and serve up.

GLASS	Rocks
GARNISH	Lemon zest
NOTABLE SUBSTITUTIONS	Rittenhouse rye, Mitcher's US*1 Single Barrel rye, Buffalo Trace Bourbon, Jefferson Reserve Bourbon

ious
infused
mple syrup
al notes
t are not
nk's original
n find them,
n place of
they bring
l fruitiness

AMERICANO

Curiously enough, the Americano was also a favorite of James Bond (it's the first drink he orders in *Casino Royale*), but it never came to be associated with the spy in the way that the Vesper and, of course, the Martini were. Its origins date back to Italy in the 1860s, when it was first called the Milano-Torino, a reference to its ingredients, Campari (from Milan) and Cinzano sweet vermouth (from Torino). The drink became wildly popular with visiting Americans, and so the drink was nicknamed the Americano. The moniker stuck, and the rest, as they say, is history. One with a bitter, orange bite.

SEIDER'S FORMULA

SPIRIT	1 ounce Campari
BITTERS	½ ounce Antica Formula sweet vermouth
SWEET	½ ounce Dolin sweet vermouth
EFFERVESENCE	Club soda

METHOD

Stir the Campari and vermouth in a chilled glass and add ice. Top with soda and stir again.

GLASS	Collins
GARNISH	Orange peel
NOTABLE SUBSTITUTIONS	Cocchi Americano, Montenegro amaro (for more delicate floral notes); Cynar (for a more herbal and bitter taste)

VIEUX CARRÉ

Like its close relative, the Sazerac, the Vieux Carré was born during the Depression in the French Quarter of New Orleans. It was first mixed by head bartender Walter Bergeron at the Hotel Monteleone, a favorite watering hole of writers such as Tennessee Williams, Truman Capote, and William Faulkner. The cocktail, according to the Hotel Monteleone, was an homage to the different ethnic groups of New Orleans' *quartier*: French (Cognac), American (rye), Italy (sweet vermouth), and Caribbean (Angostura bitters).

SEIDER'S FORMULA

AROMATIC	Averna amaro mist
SPIRIT	1 ounce Knob Creek rye
SPIRIT	1 ounce Château du Brueil Calvados
SWEET	¾ ounce Dolin sweet vermouth
BITTERS	2 dashes Peychaud's bitters
BITTERS	2 dashes Angostura bitters

METHOD

Using an atomizer, spray amaro into a chilled glass. Stir the remaining ingredients with ice in a mixing glass. Strain into chilled glass and pour over fresh ice.

GLASS	Rocks
GARNISH	Lemon zest
NOTABLE SUBSTITUTIONS	Rittenhouse rye, Jefferson Reserve Bourbon, Eagle Rare 10-year-old Bourbon, Basil Hayden (rye/Bourbon); Boulard VSOP Pays d'Auge (Calvados)

My recipe elevates the
Vieux Carré by substituting
Calvados for the Cognac,
which adds an appealing
dimension of apple and spice.
Always choose a VS, VSOP
or younger aged Calvados
because these younger spirits
have a more dominant apple
profile than aged varieties.

The traditional julep can feel flat and dimensionless.
The dash of lime juice yields a lighter, brighter
drink that will turn heads (and hats) on Derby Day.
Wheated Bourbon will make for a smoother julep;
using rye will nudge it over to the spicier side.

MINT JULEP

Nothing says languor and opulence better than the Mint Julep, which seems apropos, considering this southern classic is derived from a centuries-old Arab drink from the Mediterranean. The original recipe, which combined rose petals and water, was known as a *julab* (which means "rosewater" in Arabic). Of course, a Mint Julep sipped at the Kentucky Derby is a far cry from that non-alcoholic tincture, which was known for its life-enhancing effects. But who's to say that the Mint Julep, which has become synonymous with hospitality and literary swagger, is not life enhancing? Channel your inner Faulkner.

SEIDER'S FORMULA

SPIRIT	2½ ounces Buffalo Trace Bourbon
SWEET	¾ ounce mint-agave mix (page 138)
SOUR	¼ ounce fresh lime juice

METHOD

Shake all the ingredients with ice in a shaker tin. Double strain and pour over fresh ice.

GLASS	Rocks
GARNISH	Orange zest
NOTABLE SUBSTITUTIONS	Eagle Rare 10-year-old Bourbon, Jefferson Reserve Bourbon, Knob Creek rye

BLOOD AND SAND

The Blood and Sand is a classic Scotch cocktail. Little is known about its origins, but the first printed recipe for it appeared in *The Savoy Cocktail Book* in 1930 and was more than likely named after the 1922 film starring Rudolph Valentino, based on a book by a Spanish author named Vincente Blasco Ibáñez. Featuring equal parts orange juice, Scotch whiskey, Cherry Heering, and sweet vermouth, the drink traditionally packs a smoky, yet tropical punch.

SEIDER'S FORMULA

SPIRIT	1¾ ounces Sheep Dip Scotch
SPIRIT	¼ ounce Compass Box Peat Monster Scotch
CITRUS	¾ ounce fresh orange juice
SWEET	¾ ounce Dolin sweet vermouth
FRUIT	3 muddled Luxardo cherries
TEXTURE	¼ ounce egg white

METHOD

Shake all the ingredients with ice in a shaker tin. Double strain and pour over fresh ice.

GLASS	Rocks or double Old Fashioned
GARNISH	Luxardo cherry
NOTABLE SUBSTITUTIONS	Famous Grouse (Scotch), Chivas Regal 12-year-old; Jameson Black Irish Whiskey

ALCHEMIST NOTE

Making use of lovely Luxardo cherries instead of the usual Cherry Heering liqueur and adding a dash of Peat Monster Scotch as a modifier imparts a lavish taste with an elegant undertone of smoke, creating a perfectly balanced version of this traditionally heavy-handed drink. For a more decadent twist, I use Jameson Black, an Irish whiskey, which has a Bourbon-Scotch hybrid flavor and lush, creamy mouthfeel, with toasty oak and vanilla notes.

ALCHEMIST NOTE

Experimenting with different gins (such as a barrel-aged one) will make a significant impact on the experience of this clean and simple cocktail. Beefeater is the standard, or, in other words, the launching pad from which to explore other gins. Look for gins that, like Beefeater, are not overly piney (such as Plymouth), which allow the citrus notes of this drink to radiate and make this sometimes maligned classic feel less "ginny."

TOM COLLINS

The Tom Collins was created in the nineteenth century by the renowned bartender Jerry Thomas, who was capitalizing on a common hoax of the time. The ruse involved the invention of one Tom Collins, a loud and boisterous man who was known to sit in taverns and talk harshly of everyone he'd met, and even people he hadn't. As the story goes, friends of those who fell victim to Collins's loquacious wrath would find the unknowing victim and let him know of all the profanity directed toward him. The target was then encouraged to Collins in the bar. However, when the victim went to the tavern where Collins was meant to be, he was nowhere to be found. Fortunately, once "Professor" Thomas came on the scene, those asking for a Tom Collins would be presented with a nice fizzy cocktail of gin, lemon juice, gum syrup (a predecessor of simple syrup), and soda, and all was forgiven.

SEIDER'S FORMULA

SPIRIT	2 ounces Beefeater London Dry gin
SWEET	¾ ounce agave mix (page 136)
SOUR	¾ ounce fresh lemon juice
EFFERVESENCE	Club soda

METHOD

Shake the gin, agave mix, and lemon juice with ice in a shaker tin. Double strain and pour over fresh ice. Top with soda.

GLASS	Collins
GARNISH	Luxardo cherry
NOTABLE SUBSTITUTIONS	No.3 London Dry, Plymouth, Ford's

MOJITO

Given its popularity in the modern age, it might seem surprising that the mojito dates back to the late sixteenth century. It descends from a popular cocktail in Cuba called the Draquecito, created by a soldier of Sir Francis Drake, who, while pillaging the Caribbean, liked to sip a curious concoction of *aguardiente* (a predecessor to rum), mint, lime, and sugar. Once the Bacardí family began distilling rum, *aguardiente* was replaced by Don Facundo's spirit. This, coupled with the modern advents of soda and that lovely thing called refrigeration, gave rise to the drink we know and love today.

SEIDER'S FORMULA

SPIRIT	2 ounces Caña Brava blanco rum
SOUR	¾ ounce fresh lime juice
SWEET	¾ ounce mint-agave mix (page 138)
EFFERVESENCE	1 ounce club soda

METHOD

Shake the rum, lime juice, and mint mix with ice in a shaker tin. Add the soda. Double strain and pour over fresh ice.

GLASS	Rocks
GARNISH	Mint sprig
NOTABLE SUBSTITUTIONS	Flor de Caña 4-year blanco, Starr African Rum

ALCHEMIST NOTE

Sometimes throwing out convention leaves room for innovation. Case in point: the updated Mojito. Lose the traditional mint salad, and you let in a whole new world of flavor. You'll still get the drink's signature minty taste in the mint-infused agave mix, but without the leaves in the way you'll get a brighter, cleaner drink.

ALCHEMIST NOTE

If left with the original recipe, which calls for a total of 3 ounces of gin, Mr. Bond would be MIA and the safety of the world as we know it would be in jeopardy. Fortunately, our modern tweak of halving the gin and balancing it with Lillet and vodka keeps everyone upright for another hand of poker.

VESPER

The Vesper cocktail's first incarnation was developed at Boodle's gentlemen's club in London in the early 1950s, and called for two parts Boodle's London dry gin, one part Russian Standard vodka, and a half part Lillet Blanc. The original recipe has been somewhat obscured by the drink's popularity, counting among its fans the likes of Winston Churchill, and, of course, Ian Fleming, who featured the cocktail in his novel *Casino Royale*, a little story about a spy by the name of James Bond. Fleming named the cocktail the Vesper after Russian spy Vesper Lynd. The mixing of the gin and vodka signified the bond between the British and Russian spies. Though this pair of spies ultimately end up on opposite sides, their namesake drink has enjoyed a long, enduring history.

SEIDER'S FORMULA

SPIRIT	1½ ounces Beefeater gin
SPIRIT	1 ounce Russian Standard platinum vodka
SWEET	½ ounce Lillet Blanc

METHOD

Stir all the ingredients with ice in a mixing glass. Strain and serve up.

GLASS	Martini or coupe
GARNISH	Orange peel
NOTABLE SUBSTITUTIONS	Bombay Sapphire (London dry-style gin); No. 3, Plymouth, Brooklyn, Ford's (New American/New Western gin)

CAIPIRINHA

The Caipirinha, whose name means "little countryside drink" in Portuguese, is bound up intimately with the traditions and history surrounding its base alcohol, cachaça, the most popular Brazilian spirit. It's commonly thought that the Caipirinha evolved alongside the growth of sugarcane production during the nineteenth century. The field workers, eager for new, palatable ways to consume cachaça, would muddle limes with sugar before stirring in the liquor, and thus was the Caipirinha born. Another less-accepted version tells the tale of Portuguese slave traders returning to Europe who would use limes in their drinks to battle scurvy. It was a hell of a cocktail—and disease-fighting, too.

SEIDER'S FORMULA

SPIRIT	2 ounces Leblon cachaça
SOUR	1 ounce fresh lime juice
SWEET	¾ ounce agave mix (page 136)

METHOD

Shake all the ingredients with ice in a shaker tin. Double strain and pour over fresh ice.

GLASS	Rocks
GARNISH	Lime zest or wedge
NOTABLE SUBSTITUTIONS	Sagatiba

Forego the customary muddling of limes, which makes for a messy drink on several levels. Instead, substitute an effortless mixture of lime juice and agave, and couple it with the simple pep of essential oils from the lime-zest garnish for a fresh take on this well-worn classic.

FRENCH 75

The famous French 75 was born out of battle not of bubbly, its name a tribute to a 75-millimeter artillery gun from World War I. But more important, it was imagined as a toast to love and loss, and it sparked the imagination of weary postwar Europe. The drink inspired international experimentation among versions made with Calvados, Cognac, and finally gin. The official accepted recipe is the one that appeared in Harry Craddock's *The Savoy Cocktail Book*, and has remained a standard of bars worldwide ever since.

SEIDER'S FORMULA

SPIRIT	1 ounce Ford's gin
SWEET	¾ ounce agave mix (page 136)
SOUR	½ ounce fresh lemon juice
EFFERVESENCE	2 ounces Prosecco

METHOD

Shake the gin, agave mix, and lemon juice with ice in a shaker tin. Add the Prosecco. Double strain and serve up.

GLASS	Champagne flute
GARNISH	Lemon peel
NOTABLE SUBSTITUTIONS	No. 3 London Dry, Plymouth, Brooklyn

WHISKEY SOUR

The Whiskey Sour is the granddaddy of all sours, and was one of the recipes in Jerry Thomas's original *Bar-Tender's Guide*. It is the official drink of the 184-year-old Jefferson Literary and Debating Society at the University of Virginia, where it is rumored that a young Edgar Allen Poe was an avid fan. Nowadays, the Whiskey Sour can seem pedestrian, but, with such a long history, how can anyone leave it out of a lexicon of classic cocktails? As the original sour, it paved the way for an array of classics, both old and new.

SEIDER'S FORMULA

SPIRIT	2 ounces Jefferson Reserve
SOUR	1 ounce fresh lemon juice
SWEET	¾ ounce agave mix (page 136)
TEXTURE	Optional: ½ ounce egg white

METHOD

Shake all the ingredients (including the egg white, if using) in a shaker tin. Add ice and shake again. Double strain and pour over fresh ice.

GLASS	Rocks
GARNISH	Luxardo cherry
NOTABLE SUBSTITUTIONS	Eagle Rare 10-year-old Bourbon, Buffalo Trace Bourbon, Knob Creek rye

familiar that it may take a leap
can be elevated to anything
...otidian of drinks. But a few
do just that. Substitute the agave
...le syrup, and shake in a bit of
...re, and voilà: You've got a fresh,

GIMLET

Unlike those of many other mixed drinks, the origins of the Gimlet are clear and well documented. Sir Thomas Gimlette, a British surgeon who became the country's surgeon general, invented the Gimlet in the late nineteenth century as a way to stave off scurvy among British sailors. The Merchant Shipping Act of 1867 required all ships of the British military and merchant fleet to provide sailors with a regular dose of lime juice—leading to the nickname "limey" for English immigrants in the early British colonies. By the time the act was passed, Lauchlin Rose had patented a method for preserving citrus juice in a sugar syrup without alcohol, and the result was Rose's lime juice. Gimlette persuaded his fellow seamen to drink the required amount of lime juice by adding a third magical ingredient: gin. Nowadays, however, vodka is an acceptable and equally popular choice to mix into this classic.

SEIDER'S FORMULA

SPIRIT	2 ounces Beefeater gin (or Russian Standard vodka)
SOUR	1 ounce fresh lime juice
SWEET	¾ ounce agave mix (page 136)

METHOD

Shake all the ingredients with ice in a mixing glass. Double strain and serve up.

GLASS	Double Old Fashioned
GARNISH	Lime zest
NOTABLE SUBSTITUTIONS	No. 3 (gin); Aylesbury Duck, Brooklyn Republic, Boyd & Blair, Karlsson's (vodka)

COSMOPOLITAN

Most people agree that a Cosmopolitan appeared on the West Coast of America at some point during the 1980s, and traveled from there to New York and beyond. However, Cheryl Cook claims to have invented the drink during the latter half of the 1980s while working as the head bartender of the Strand on Washington Avenue in South Beach, Miami. She apparently based her drink on the newly available Absolut Citron vodka and added a splash of triple sec, a dash of Rose's lime juice, and, in her own words, "just enough cranberry to make it oh-so pretty in pink." Her version traveled to Manhattan, where Toby Cecchini is credited with being the first to use fresh lime juice in place of Rose's at his bar, Passerby. A likely early ancestor of the Cosmopolitan is the Harpoon, a drink promoted by Ocean Spray during the 1960s that consisted of vodka, cranberry juice, and a squeeze of fresh lime. And a long-forgotten 1934 book of gin recipes, *Pioneers of Mixing Gin at Elite Bars*, contains a recipe that is very similar to today's drink, only with lemon in place of lime, gin in place of vodka, and raspberry juice in place of cranberry.

SEIDER'S FORMULA

SPIRIT	2 ounces Russian Standard vodka
SWEET	¾ ounce agave mix (page 136)
TART	¾ ounce cranberry juice
SOUR	½ ounce fresh lime juice
BITTERS	2 dashes orange bitters

METHOD

Shake all the ingredients with ice in a mixing glass. Double strain and serve up.

ALCHEMIST NOTE

Most flavored vodkas
taste artificial, so I opt for
unflavored unless you make
an infusion yourself with
fresh citrus peel (see page
140). The ratio of vodka to
equal parts agave mix and
cranberry juice with just a
little less lime juice makes
for a nice balance of sweet
and sour.

GLASS	Martini or coupe
GARNISH	Lemon peel (pinch and discard)
NOTABLE SUBSTITUTIONS	If you don't have agave mix on hand, you may substitute Cointreau or another good-quality orange cordial. Try to avoid triple sec, as it has a cloying flavor.

ALCHEMIST NOTE

The standard Dark and Stormy
can be flat and very sweet, with
no layers of flavor to add zing.
This recipe flips the original
on its head. Replacing syrupy
ginger beer with a combination
of allspice mix and a sprinkle of
cinnamon and pepper creates a
bolder flavor without sacrificing
the drink's crucial ability to
refresh. You can top with ginger
beer for that authentic Dark and
Stormy flavor, or use club soda
for a cleaner taste.

DARK AND STORMY

Like the drink itself, the origins of the Dark and Stormy are somewhat murky. We begin on the high seas with a bottle of navy-strength dark rum, a type of high-proof dark rum enjoyed by British sailors as part of their rations during the nineteenth century. Around 1860, a company called Gosling Bros., of Hamilton, Bermuda, began bottling a version of this "old rum"; others in the area were, at the same time, brewing a new drink called "ginger beer." Ginger beer was possibly an attempt at temperance, but instead of choosing one of over the other, imbibers enjoyed these two homegrown beverages together, bringing us the maritime-themed cocktail we know today.

SEIDER'S FORMULA

SPIRIT	2 ounces Gosling's rum
SOUR	½ ounce fresh lime juice
SWEET/SPICE	½ ounce five-spice agave mix (page 138)
EFFERVESENCE	Ginger beer or club soda

METHOD

Shake the rum, lime juice, and five-spice agave mix with ice in a shaker tin. Double strain and pour over fresh ice. Top with ginger beer.

GLASS	Collins
GARNISH	Lime zest, freshly grated ginger
NOTABLE SUBSTITUTIONS	You have to use Goslings to call your drink a Dark and Stormy. But if you want a similar, less spicy drink, you can substitute Blackwell rum or Bacareli 8-year. Then add a dash or two of Angostura bitters to give it a touch of aromatics and spice.

Hawthorne
Strainer

Tea
Strainer

LARGE
SHAKER

Small
Shaker

Tincture

Jigger

Spice

Sour

Herb

Fruit

ALCHEMY

GROUND TO GLASS

> **SUMMIT BAR**

The Ground to Glass was born on a rooftop where my brother and I grew a cornucopia of vegetables (much to the chagrin of our landlord) and used them to tweak the classic Margarita. Our Bloody Mary-Margarita hybrid features red pepper and cucumber, highlighted by the earthy vegetable notes of tequila. For an added dimension of BBQ-influenced umami, I topped it with hickory smoked salt, thus crowning our pilgrimage from ground to glass.

FOUNDATION

SPIRIT	2 ounces Corralejo blanco tequila
SOUR	1 ounce fresh lime juice, and lime wedge
SWEET	¾ ounce agave mix (page 136)

DIMENSION

GARDEN	1 cucumber slice
GARDEN	¾ ounce red pepper puree (page 146)
BITTERS	2 dashes orange bitters

FINISH

SPICE/TEXTURE	Hickory smoked salt (page 165)

METHOD

Rub the top rim of the glass with the lime wedge, then roll in smoked salt. Muddle the cucumber in a shaker tin. Add all the remaining ingredients and shake with ice. Double strain and pour over fresh ice.

GLASS	Double Old Fashioned
NOTABLE SUBSTITUTIONS	Olmeca Altos, Herradura, and Cabeza Blanco

ALCHEMIST NOTE
Steer clear of añejo tequilas, as barrel age drowns out the brightness of the drink. Younger blanco tequilas like Corralejo have an earthy vegetal quality and a slight citrus finish that awaken the palate in a Margarita-style cocktail.

NIKITA BAY BREEZE

▶ NIKITA

To this day, one of my summertime guilty pleasures is ordering a Malibu Bay Breeze. One of my business partners, Jeremie Kittredge, says it tastes like drinking Coppertone suntan lotion in a glass. And that's why I like it: The smell and flavor throw me back to being a kid and getting that first whiff of hot sand and candied coconut on the beach. When I started the project at Nikita in Malibu I was, of course, compelled to create my own version of the Malibu Bay Breeze. To re-create the coconut rum, I took shredded coconut, toasted it, and infused it into a blend of rums. I then took fresh pineapple puree, added some Vietnamese cinnamon agave to give it an exotic spice, and brought it all together with homemade spiced cranberry bitters. Fresh lime juice provided a bright citrus body, and the garnish of toasted coconut and aromatics from fresh lime zest transformed this punchline of a drink into a sophisticated cocktail.

ALCHEMIST NOTE

I like to use an equal blend of two rums to make the infusion for this drink. The fresh sugarcane citrus notes of the Caña Brava balance the darker, richer fruit and spice flavors of the Flor de Cana 7-year.

FOUNDATION

SPIRIT	2 ounces toasted coconut-infused rum (page 141)
SOUR	½ ounce fresh lime juice

DIMENSION

SPICE/FRUIT/ SWEET	1½ ounces cinnamon pineapple puree (page 146)

FINISH

BITTERS	2 dashes spiced cranberry bitters (page 143)
AROMATIC	Lime zest
TEXTURE	Toasted coconut

METHOD

Shake the rum, lime juice, pineapple puree, and bitters with ice in a shaker tin. Double strain and pour over fresh ice. Sprinkle the top of the drink with lime zest and toasted coconut.

GLASS	Large rocks or double Old Fashioned
NOTABLE SUBSTITUTIONS	Flor de Cana 4-year-old extra dry, Old New Orleans 3-year-old, Bacardi 8-year

ALCHEMIST NOTE
Old Raj is infused with saffron as well as juniper, citrus, nuts and, spices, and it maintains its complexity despite being 110 proof. Rothman & Winter Orchard apricot liqueur has a ripe, fresh orchard fruit flavor and bouquet and an elegant, long finish.

ORIGIN: Vesper (Spirit + Sour [Acid] + Sweet)
ELEVATION: Acid + Fruit + Floral + Tincture + Spice + Texture

THE APOLOGY

SUMMIT BAR

The Apology is an evolution, or, better still, an elevation of the great Vesper cocktail of Bond lore. Ousting Lillet for the complex French oak tones of Chardonnay, this drink combines the latter with high-proof, saffron-infused Cadenhead's Old Raj gin, a fruity apricot cordial, and the flowery finish of St. Germain. The Apology is the cocktail equivalent of a bouquet of flowers, the ultimate "get out of the doghouse" free card, a wink, and an ode to the forgotten art of chivalry.

FOUNDATION

SPIRIT	1 ounce Cadenhead's Old Raj gin, 110 proof
ACID	2 ounces Chardonnay

DIMENSION

FRUIT	1 ounce Rothman & Winter Orchard apricot liqueur
FLORAL/SWEET	¼ ounce St. Germain liqueur

FINISH

BITTERS/SPICE	2 dashes saffron tincture (page 144)
SWEET/TEXTURE	Bourbon-soaked apricot (page 145)

METHOD

Stir the gin, wine, liqueurs, and bitters with ice in a mixing glass. Strain and serve up. Garnish with apricot skewer.

GLASS	Martini or coupe
NOTABLE SUBSTITUTIONS	Cadenhead's 92, Bombay Sapphire

MLC

▶ **LE BERNARDIN**

The MLC is an ode to Maguy Le Coze, cofounder of Le Bernardin in New York. I was brought in to develop the cocktail program for Le Coze and her chef, Eric Ripert. Collaborating with Eric was an unforgettable experience, as I was given the opportunity to explore complex flavor combinations with curious culinary-inspired ingredients, using menu items as launching points for my creations. The drink was roused by my love of Eric's poached escolar scented with kaffir lime and lemongrass. The MLC, a Margarita-inspired libation, features four different iterations of kaffir lime: agave, tincture, infused Maldon sea salt, and a leaf garnish. Each element has a flavor key to the uniqueness of the drink. The agave introduces this exotic lime flavor with sweetness. The tincture reinforces the delicate finish of agave and keeps the mouthfeel bright, while the Maldon sea salt balances the sweetness of the agave and has a flakier crunch and more satisfying texture than the usual kosher salt.

FOUNDATION

SPIRIT	2 ounces Cabeza blanco tequila
SOUR	1 ounce fresh lime juice, plus lime wedge
SWEET	¾ ounce agave mix (page 136)

DIMENSION

EXOTIC/ TINCTURE	2 dashes kaffir lime tincture (page 144)

FINISH

TEXTURE	Kaffir lime salt (page 145)
AROMATIC	Kaffir lime leaf

METHOD

Rub the top rim of the glass with the lime wedge, then roll in kaffir lime salt. Shake the tequila, lime juice, agave mix, and tincture with ice in a shaker tin. Double strain and pour over fresh ice. Garnish with the kaffir lime leaf.

GLASS	Double Old Fashioned
NOTABLE SUBSTITUTIONS	Corralejo Blanco Arte nom 1414, Olmeca Altos

TEQUILA MOCKING BIRD

▸ **SUMMIT BAR**

Born in summer, not unlike the long hot season of struggle depicted in Harper Lee's work, Tequila Mocking Bird is a drink that thrives on the rich energy of contrasts. The sweetness of pineapple plays off the zing of citrus. Jalapeño bounces off the earthiness of tequila, and cardamom adds an unexpected wow factor to an already unusual composite of flavors. Diversity in a glass.

FOUNDATION

SPIRIT	2 ounces Olmeca Altos blanco tequila
SOUR	½ ounce fresh lime juice
SWEET	½ ounce agave mix (page 136)

DIMENSION

FRUIT/PIQUANT	1½ ounces jalapeño pineapple puree (page 146)
BITTERS	1 dash Scrappy's cardamom bitters

FINISH

EFFERVESCENCE	Splash of club soda
SPICE/AROMATIC	Ground cardamom
GARNISH	Pineapple leaf

METHOD

Shake the tequila, lime juice, agave mix, pineapple puree, and bitters with ice in a shaker tin. Add the club soda. Double strain and pour over fresh ice. Sprinkle ground cardamom on top. Garnish with pineapple leaf.

GLASS	Collins
NOTABLE SUBSTITUTION	Corralejo Blanco Arte nom 1414

BREAKING THE LAW

▸ SUMMIT BAR

My friend Stephen Myers introduced me to Ilegal before mezcal was widely available in bars, let alone common in cocktails. He entertained me with stories of the "old days" when Ilegal's owner, John Rexer, would smuggle it on rafts from Mexico to his bar in Guatemala. Inspired by this tall tale of taste and adventure, I paired the renegade spirit with a floral, grappa-like cordial called Dimmi, lengthening the flavor of smoke from the mezcal. I then added chipotle-infused agave for a smoky-sweet spice, then cooled the whole thing down with cucumber and lime juice, releasing my own little bandit for illicit consumption.

ALCHEMIST NOTE

I like Ilegal, as it exhibits nice terroir and has a more balanced smokiness than other mezcals, but it can be a bit pricey for everyday use. For a nice alternative, Don Amado has a smooth, soft smoke, which allows the earthiness of agave to shine through. You can also substitute a blanco (plata or joven) or a reposado, but make sure the the mezcal is smooth and not overly smoky, so as not to mask the other flavors.

FOUNDATION

SPIRIT	1 ounce Ilegal mezcal (joven or reposado)
SWEET/FLORAL	1 ounce Dimmi Italian cordial
SOUR	¾ ounce fresh lime juice

DIMENSION

GARDEN	1 slice cucumber
SWEET/PIQUANT	¾ ounce chipotle chile agave mix (page 137)
BITTERS	2 dashes Scrappy's orange bitters (page 165)

FINISH

EFFERVESCENCE	Splash of club soda
AROMATIC	Lime zest

METHOD

Muddle the cucumber in a shaker tin. Add the mezcal, cordial, lime juice, agave mix, and bitters and shake with ice. Add the club soda. Double strain and pour over fresh ice. Garnish with lime zest sprinkled over top.

GLASS	Collins
NOTABLE SUBSTITUTIONS	Don Amado, Mina Real, Fidencio, Del Maguey Vida

ALCHEMIST NOTE
Opt for a bright gin with plenty of citrus notes. Avoid classic London dry gin, piney gin, or a gin with too many botanicals, as they are too heavy in this delicate drink.

LB CHAMPAGNE COCKTAIL

▸ **LE BERNARDIN**

The LB was born out of my passion for a particular dish at Le Bernardin. I wanted an elegant Champagne cocktail to pair with an especially delicious lobster dish that piqued my interest with its peculiar lemongrass flavor. With the slight spice of black peppercorn agave, the vivid citrus of No. 3 gin and fresh lemon juice, and the Champagne's effervescence, the LB elevated the richness of the lobster, allowing more of the flavors to linger on the palate. But this drink's no snob. Like her graceful older sister, the LB makes pleasant company before or during just about any meal.

FOUNDATION

SPIRIT	1 ounce No. 3 gin
SOUR	½ ounce fresh lemon juice

DIMENSION

SWEET/SPICE	¾ ounce lemongrass peppercorn agave mix (page 138)

FINISH

TINCTURE	2 dashes lemongrass peppercorn tincture (page 144)
EFFERVESCENCE	3 ounces Champagne
AROMATIC	Lemon peel

METHOD

Shake the gin, lemon juice, agave mix, and tincture with ice in a shaker tin. Add Champagne. Double strain and serve up. Garnish with spiral of lemon peel.

GLASS	Champagne flute
NOTABLE SUBSTITUTIONS	Brooklyn, Spring 44, Bombay Sapphire East

FRENCH CONNECTION

▸ LE BERNARDIN

Despite the name (a reference to Le Bernardin's French heritage), this drink
is based on a popular English aperitif, the Pimm's Cup, the perfect elixir to
whet the taste buds before a meal. But when you're at Le Bernardin, you're
not preparing the palate for just any meal. I needed a take on a classic that
would be a clean preamble to the intricacies of a typical plate at Le Bernardin.
I opted for a five-spice agave mix that brought out the unique blend of flavors
in the Pimm's and used yuzu, a Japanese citrus fruit, over the usual lime, which
adds a bright floral note. I then sealed the proverbial deal with a kiss of anise by
atomizing the glass with a gentle mist of absinthe.

ALCHEMIST NOTE

When making a tall drink with
a sparkling wine or soda, your
shake should be shorter than
with other cocktails because
the soda will dilute the drink,
as does the ice in the shaker.

FOUNDATION

SPIRIT	2 ounces Pimm's No. 1
SOUR	¼ ounce yuzu juice

DIMENSION

GARDEN	1 slice cucumber
SWEET/SPICE	1 ounce five-spice agave mix (page 138)
BITTERS	1 dash orange bitters
BITTERS	1 dash Angostora bitters

FINISH

AROMATIC	Absinthe mist
EFFERVESCENCE	3 ounces club soda
SPICE	3 whole star anise

METHOD

Using an atomizer, mist the glass with absinthe. Muddle the cucumber in a shaker tin. Add the Pimm's, yuzu juice, agave mix, and orange and Angostura bitters and shake with ice. Add the club soda. Double strain and pour over fresh ice.

GLASS	Highball or Collins
NOTABLE SUBSTITUTIONS	Equal parts lemon, lime, and grapefruit juices (for the yuzu)

APEROL NOIR

▸ **LE BERNARDIN**

The wine program at Le Bernardin is a thing of beauty, as diverse and daring as one can imagine. I showcased this largesse in a pre-dinner offering called the Aperol Noir, which uses Pinot Noir as an accent in a sexy, visually dramatic drink. Its bright berry fruit pairs well with Aperol's rhubarb-orange spice profile. The citrus offsets the Aperol's sweetness and gives the drink body and dimension.

FOUNDATION

SPIRIT	1 ounce Aperol
SOUR	¼ ounce fresh lemon juice
EFFERVESCENCE	3 ounces sparkling wine

DIMENSION

SWEET/SPICE	1 ounce Pinot Noir black pepper agave mix (page 139)
BITTERS	2 dashes orange bitters

FINISH

FRUIT/TANNIN	Float (½ ounce) Pinot Noir
AROMATIC	Orange zest

METHOD

Shake the Aperol, lemon juice, agave mix, and bitters with ice in a shaker tin. Add the sparkling wine. Double strain and pour over fresh ice. Place a spoon over the center of the glass and pour the wine over the spoon. Sprinkle orange zest over the top of the drink.

GLASS	Collins or highball
NOTABLE SUBSTITUTIONS	Gran Classico Bitter

THE LAST COCKTAIL

▶ **PRIMA**

I penned my first cocktail book for the Luxury Collection Hotel and Resorts, with Francis Harris from Pravda, the subterranean Russian bar in Manhattan. We found inspiration in the Collection's global properties to create an array of signature cocktails. Like a brisk drive through the Italian countryside, the Last Cocktail takes your breath away with juniper, pear, rosemary, the pep of fresh lemon juice, crisp bubbles of Prosecco, and a curious finish of clove. Once you've had one, it's the only (last) thing you'll ever want to drink.

FOUNDATION

SPIRIT	1 ounce No. 3 gin
SOUR	1 ounce fresh lemon juice

DIMENSION

FRUIT/SWEET/HERB	2 ounces pear rosemary puree (page 146)
EFFERVESCENCE	1½ ounces Prosecco

FINISH

SPICE/AROMATIC	Ground clove
HERB	Fresh rosemary sprig

METHOD

Shake the gin, lemon juice, and pear-rosemary puree with ice in a shaker tin. Add the Prosecco. Double strain and pour over fresh ice. Sprinkle ground clove on top and garnish with the rosemary sprig.

GLASS	Rocks, double Old Fashioned, Martini, coupe
NOTABLE SUBSTITUTIONS	Bombay Sapphire East, Spring 44, Brooklyn

ALCHEMIST NOTE
Choosing an overly piney gin will throw off the rosemary and clove notes that are essential to this drink. Substituting Champagne for Prosecco is not recommended, as the dry notes in Prosecco are needed to give the drink a crisp pop.

51ST STREET MANHATTAN

▸ LE BERNARDIN

At Le Bernardin, I wanted to create cocktails that spoke a three-Michelin-star vernacular. Aldo Sohm, Le Bernardin's sommelier, introduced me to this remarkable Madeira. It had a slight dryness and a long, subtle, nutty finish. This was the cornerstone around which I built an updated Manhattan. I infused rye with my favorite ginger rooibos tea from Rare Tea Cellar and combined this with the Madeira to create a spiced floral nuttiness that complements the subtle botanicals of the vermouth.

FOUNDATION

SPIRIT/SPICE/TEA	Ginger rooibos-infused rye (page 140)
SWEET	1½ ounces Dolin sweet vermouth

DIMENSION

TEA/TINCTURE	2 dashes rooibos tincture (page 144)
BITTERS	2 dashes orange bitters

FINISH

EXOTIC	⅛ ounce Charleston Madeira
SWEET/GARNISH	Madeira-soaked cherry (page 145)

METHOD

Swirl Madeira in the glass to coat the inside. Do not discard. Stir the tea, vermouth, tincture, and bitters with ice in a mixing glass. Strain into the glass and serve up. Garnish with the Madeira-soaked cherry.

GLASS	Martini or coupe
NOTABLE SUBSTITUTIONS	Rittenhouse, Jefferson's Reserve, Knob Creek

Charleston Madeira is very
dry but still has enough
nuttiness to balance out
the heat of the rye and the
floral notes from Dolin sweet
vermouth. If you can't get a
hold of it, choose a Madeira
that is not too full bodied
or sweet. For the rye, any
overproof selection will do.

EL MATADOR

▸ NIKITA

While driving up the coast to Santa Barbara, I was overtaken with an overwhelming feeling of serenity as I stared out on the seemingly endless beaches of southern California. I stopped my car, got out, looked over the soaring bluff of El Matador, and inspiration struck. The coast is a destination, and nothing says vacation better than a Margarita. But scenery this inspired demanded that I take it up a notch. As it happened, I was on my way to see my supplier of kaffir lime leaves, and I started thinking about how to work those into my elevated Margarita. First element: a bright blanco tequila. I chose Olmeco Altos, added the usual proportion of lime. Then I infused agave with hibiscus tea, imparting a subtle tannin to the texture of the drink. Last and certainly not least, the final touch of the very kaffir lime leaves that brought me up the coast on the day of my inspiration, in three forms: bitters, salt, and the leaf itself. El Matador, olé!

ALCHEMIST NOTE

Kaffir lime leaves can be found in most Asian specialty stores, either frozen or fresh. Once you buy them, keep them in your own freezer, tightly wrapped, so you'll always have them on hand.

FOUNDATION

SPIRIT	2 ounces Olmeco Altos blanco tequila
SOUR	¾ ounce fresh lime juice

DIMENSION

SWEET/TEA	¾ ounce hibiscus-infused agave mix (page 138)

FINISH

SOUR	Lime wedge
EXOTIC/TEXTURE	Kaffir lime salt (page 145)
BITTERS	3 dashes kaffir lime tincture (page 144)
AROMATIC	Lime zest
AROMATIC/ EXOTIC	Smacked kaffir lime leaf

METHOD

Moisten half of the rim of the glass with the lime wedge. Holding the glass at a slight angle, roll the moistened edge in kaffir lime salt. Fill the glass with ice. Shake the tequila, lime juice, agave mix, and bitters with ice in a shaker tin. Double strain into the glass. Sprinkle the top of the drink with lime zest and garnish with a smacked kaffir lime leaf.

GLASS	Large rocks or double Old Fashioned
NOTABLE SUBSTITUTIONS	Cabeza, Corralejo blanco, Sauza Tres Generaciones

THE MANCINI

▸ **PRIMA**

The Mancini is a tip of the hat to David Mancini, director of operations at Le Bernardin, whose family is from the same town in which Meletti Amaro is produced. David loves his Old Fashioneds, so I created this drink as an homage to the old neighborhood, so to speak. Meletti is the ideal herbal liqueur for my updated Old Fashioned, as it has enough sweetness to allow you to leave out a sugar component entirely. Meletti botanicals are infused by a singular percolation method, similar to brewing coffee, bringing out the aromatics of violet and saffron, which combines with the spice of bitters and blends smoothly with the rye. Add a pop of citrus on the finish and you have an Old Fashioned for the ages.

FOUNDATION

SPIRIT	2 ounces Mitcher's US*1 rye

DIMENSION

SWEET/HERB	½ ounce Meletti amaro

FINISH

SPICE/BITTERS	2 dashes cinnamon bitters (page 143)
BITTERS	1 dash orange bitters
AROMATIC/ GARNISH	Orange peel

METHOD

Stir the rye, amaro, and cinnamon and orange bitters with ice in a mixing glass. Strain and pour over fresh ice. Garnish with orange peel.

GLASS	Rocks
NOTABLE SUBSTITUTIONS	Rittenhouse (rye); Gran Classico Bitter (amaro)

ORIGIN: Tom Collins (Spirit + Sour + Sweet + Effervescence)
ELEVATION: Spice + Fruit + Bitters + Aromatic

SHU JAM FIZZ

▶ SUMMIT BAR

Shu Jam Fizz was the drink that put Summit on the map. It was the first drink of ours to generate a lot of press, and it was an instant hit that's still popular today. But I can't take all the credit for it since there was a customer who had a hand in its creation: Carmen Chappetta, aka Shu. It was a late summer night. I had just made a batch of fennel-infused agave with which I was going to tweak a Tom Collins. Enter stage left: Shu bearing a gift, her grandma's apricot jam. On a whim, I added a gentle spoonful of jam to my newborn Collins and, like magic, it bound all the flavors together, its sweetness rounding out the acid of the lemon juice, the citrus, pine, and black peppercorn notes of the gin, and the pop of peach bitters. The finishing note is the spray of absinthe mist, which puts the Shu Jam Fizz into full throttle, ready for the spotlight.

ALCHEMIST NOTE
Choose a jam or preserve made with only real fruit, pectin, and sugar. Steer clear of any jam with high-fructose corn syrup. Dried apricots can be substituted for Bourbon-soaked ones, if you haven't made those ahead.

FOUNDATION

SPIRIT	2 ounces Plymouth gin
SOUR	¾ ounce fresh lemon juice

DIMENSION

SWEET/SPICE	¾ ounce fennel-infused agave mix (page 137)
FRUIT	2 barspoons (or 2 teaspoons) peach jam
BITTERS	2 dashes peach bitters

FINISH

EFFERVESCENCE	1 ounce club soda
AROMATIC	Absinthe mist
FRUIT/GARNISH	Bourbon-soaked apricot skewer (page 145)

METHOD

Using an atomizer, mist the glass with absinthe. Fill the glass with ice. Shake the gin, lemon juice, agave mix, jam, and bitters with ice in a shaker tin. Add the club soda. Double strain and pour into the glass. Garnish with Bourbon-soaked apricot skewer.

GLASS	Collins or highball
NOTABLE SUBSTITUTIONS	No. 3 London Dry, Ford's, Bombay Sapphire East

OFF TO THE RACES

▸ **SUMMIT BAR**

On a balmy spring day, I received an exciting blend from my boy Rod of Rare Tea Cellar: peach blossom rooibos. It had a vibrant nose and floral flavor, with a freshness that tasted as if it had just been picked off a tree. As it happened, it was Derby day, and mint juleps were on my mind. I infused Bourbon with the tea, which balanced the heat and spice of the spirit, substituted cinnamon-like shiso as a twist on the julep's mint, and incorporated fresh lime for a cooling shot of citrus. Finally, in honor of another of the South's great traditions, I gave a nod to barbeque with a dash of chipotle tincture. Off to the races we go!

FOUNDATION

SPIRIT/TEA	2 ounces Georgia Peach Nectar Rooibos-infused Bourbon (page 140)
SOUR	1 ounce fresh lime juice

DIMENSION/POP

SWEET/HERB	¾ ounce shiso-infused agave mix (page 139)
PIQUANT/TINCTURE	2 dashes chipotle tincture (page 143)

FINISH

HERB	Smacked shiso leaves

METHOD

Shake the Bourbon, lime juice, agave mix, and tincture with ice in a shaker tin. Double strain and pour over fresh ice. Garnish with smacked shiso leaves.

GLASS	Large rocks or double Old Fashioned
NOTABLE SUBSTITUTIONS	Eagle Rare 10, Jefferson Reserve, Buffalo Trace, Elijah Craig 12-year-old

SAY HELLO TO MY LITTLE FRIEND

▶ SUMMIT BAR

When Agwa de Bolivia coca leaf liqueur came on the market, the company offered a curious point of sale (a little accessory used to help identify specific brands): a small vial of food-grade lime powder, which, when taken on the tongue, activated the alkaloids of the coca leaf. One infamous night, a friend of mine was visiting Summit Bar, and we were partaking in our poison of choice. This time, it was Agwa de Bolivia. Suddenly, across the bar, in a moment of spirit-driven dramatic inspiration, John tapped his inner Al Pacino, and took the lime powder through his nose, à la Scarface. In the spirit of that moment, "Say Hello to My Little Friend" was born. Like a bastard child of the Tom Collins, this offbeat concoction substitutes 1 ounce of Agwa for half of the gin, adding an herbaceous grassy flavor with citrus and spice notes. A couple dashes of grapefruit bitters pulls it all together under a curious umbrella of fresh botanicals.

ALCHEMIST NOTE

Grapefruit bitters are a great way to brighten up any citrus-based cocktail. Beefeater 24 works perfectly with the bitters, as it is a citrus-forward gin, without the piney taste of many other gins. Under no circumstances do we recommend snorting food-grade lime powder through your nose!

FOUNDATION

SPIRIT	1 ounce Beefeater 24 gin
SPIRIT	1 ounce Agwa de Bolivia coca leaf liqueur
SOUR	¾ ounce fresh lime juice
SWEET	¾ ounce agave mix (page 136)

DIMENSION

BITTERS	2 dashes grapefruit bitters

FINISH

EFFERVESCENCE	Splash of club soda
AROMATIC	Orange peel

METHOD

Shake the gin, liqueur, lemon juice, agave mix, and bitters with ice in a shaker tin. Add the club soda. Double strain and pour over fresh ice. Garnish with orange peel.

GLASS	Large rocks, Collins, or highball
NOTABLE SUBSTITUTIONS	Plymouth, No. 3 London Dry, Spring 44, Brooklyn

ALCHEMIST NOTE
For this drink, use a Scotch that is
soft on the palate and lightly peated,
to avoid overwhelming the sweet
honey notes of the honeybush tea.

BORN AND RAISED

▶ SUMMIT BAR

While deep in the trenches creating cocktails for the Luxury Collection, I worked alongside Meredith Dichter. It was Meredith's idea to do a cocktail book for the hotel group, and she loves Scotch, as well as the classic Scotch cocktail the Rob Roy, otherwise known as the Scotch cousin to the Manhattan. In her honor, I re-created this cocktail and put my own spin on it, choosing a honeybush tea, robust with fruity sweetness and a toasty finish, to infuse with Scotch. Dolin sweet vermouth adds a second layer of botanicals, reinforcing those already present in the tea. Meredith is from New York—"born and raised"—which became the name of a cocktail that's never out of place.

FOUNDATION

SPIRIT/TEA	2 ounces Honeybush-Infused Scotch (page 141)

DIMENSION

SWEET	½ ounce Dolin sweet vermouth
SWEET	¼ ounce agave mix (page 136)
BITTERS	2 dashes orange bitters

FINISH

AROMATIC/ GARNISH	Lemon and orange peel

METHOD

Stir the tea-infused Scotch, vermouth, agave mix, and bitters with ice in a mixing glass. Strain and pour over fresh ice. Garnish with lemon and orange peel.

GLASS	Rocks
NOTABLE SUBSTITUTION	Highland Park 12-year-old, Glenrothes Select Reserve

THE SITUATION

▶ SUMMIT BAR

The Situation alludes to my beginnings in New York, when I worked at the Mercer Kitchen. The name stood for two things: It was what I called any cocktail I created on the fly, and it was also what my friend Hamid and I called "special customers" in the room, usually of the female type. ("See the situation at table twenty?") Now on the menu at Summit, the Situation is a personal history of my taste. I've always loved rye and raisin bread, so I took Afghani raisins (a gift from Hamid's mother), and infused rye with them, using the dry heat of the spirit to bring out the flavor of the raisins. Then I added lemon juice, caraway-infused agave, orange bitters, and Fee Brothers Whiskey Barrel-Aged bitters, shook it up, sprinkled ground caraway seeds over the glass, and garnished it rye-soaked raisins. One sip and I was transported back to my childhood, my mouth full of my favorite flavors from this rye-soaked, raisin-infused situation.

ALCHEMIST NOTE
Golden raisins or
sultanas work perfectly
well in the infusion, but
if you can find Afghani
raisins, try those.

FOUNDATION

SPIRIT/FRUIT	2 ounces raisin-infused rye (page 141)
SOUR	scant 1 ounce fresh lemon juice

DIMENSION

SWEET/SPICE	1 ounce caraway-infused agave mix (page 137)
BITTERS	3 big dashes orange bitters
BITTERS	1 dash Fee Brothers Whiskey Barrel–Aged bitters (page 165)

FINISH

AROMATIC/SPICE	Ground caraway seeds
SWEET/GARNISH	Rye-soaked raisin skewer (page 145)

METHOD

Shake the rye, lemon juice, agave mix, and bitters with ice in a shaker tin. Double strain and pour over fresh ice. Sprinkle the top of the drink with ground caraway and garnish with the raisin skewer.

GLASS	Double Old Fashioned
NOTABLE SUBSTITUTIONS	Knob Creek, Bulleit, Mitcher's US*1 Straight

ALCHEMIST NOTE

Combining equal parts Bourbon and Averna in a bottle beforehand saves time and can make you feel like a true Alchemist. Make sure you get ginger beer made with fresh, natural ingredients. You don't want to be left with an artificial flavor as you sip on this tasty cocktail.

THE ROOT'S BEER

▸ **SUMMIT BAR**

The Root's Beer is my adult take on a classic American beverage. It's an unusual blend of ginger beer, vanilla notes from ZU Bison Grass vodka, and agave, balanced against a blend of Averna amaro and Bourbon, lemon juice, and a dash of sarsaparilla and orange bitters. It's a complex concoction that evokes a simple emotion, reminding us that being a grown-up isn't as easy as it once looked.

FOUNDATION

SPIRIT	1 ounce ZU Bison Grass vodka
SOUR	¼ ounce fresh lemon juice

DIMENSION

SPIRIT	1 ounce ROOT organic liqueur
SPIRIT	⅛ ounce Averna amaro–Bourbon blend
SWEET/SPICE	½ ounce black pepper–ginger agave mix (page 137)
EFFERVESCENCE	2 ounces Maine Root ginger beer

FINISH

BITTERS	1 dash orange bitters
BITTERS	2 dashes sarsaparilla bitters

METHOD

Swirl the amaro-Bourbon blend in the glass. Do not discard. Fill the glass with ice. Shake the vodka, lemon juice, agave mix, and bitters with ice in a shaker tin. Add the ginger beer. Double strain and pour into glass.

GLASS	Collins
NOTABLE SUBSTITUTION	Fever-Tree ginger beer

THE JOHN LEE HOOKER

▸ **SUMMIT BAR**

I've always loved John Lee Hooker's cover of that song *One Bourbon, One Scotch, One Beer*, but I always thought to myself, how the hell do you get it all in one glass? It made for some serious inspiration and, with a little elbow grease, the John Lee Hooker was incarnated as a cocktail in the East Village. Bourbon was the easy part. It made for a simple yet effective base. Next came the Scotch, Compass Box Peat Monster, which accented the palette of my new invention. The usual direct peat in the mouth would have been too intense, but the Peat Monster had soft, smoky notes that mixed well with the Bourbon. Before getting to John's last vice, I added Vietnamese cinnamon agave, fresh lemon juice, and a dash of sarsaparilla and orange bitters to give a mid-palate highlight. Then it was time for the party. I shook that son of a bitch up, strained it into an ice-cold beer glass, and topped it with Lagunitas Hop Stoopid beer, which added a mild bitterness. Boom! Boom! Boom! That's a bad-ass drink!

ALCHEMIST NOTE
If you can't find Hop Stoopid, you can use any double IPA that is heavily dry-hopped and aromatic.

FOUNDATION

SPIRIT	2 ounces Jefferson's Reserve Bourbon
SOUR	½ ounce fresh lemon juice

DIMENSION

SWEET/SPICE	1 ounce Vietnamese cinnamon agave mix (page 139)
BITTERS	1 dash orange bitters
BITTERS	1 dash sarsaparilla bitters

FINISH

HOPS	1½ ounces Hop Stoopid double IPA beer
AROMATIC	2 mists of Compass Box Peat Monster Scotch
AROMATIC/ GARNISH	Orange peel

METHOD

Using an atomizer, mist the glass with Scotch. Fill the glass with ice. Shake the Bourbon, lemon juice, agave mix, and bitters with ice in a shaker tin. Add the beer. Double strain and pour into the glass. Garnish with orange peel, and mist the top of the drink with a second spray of Scotch.

GLASS	Beer or pilsner
NOTABLE SUBSTITUTIONS	Eagle Rare 10-year-old, Basil Hayden's (Bourbon); Laphroaig, Lagavulin (Scotch)

CHARMANE STAR

▶ **SUMMIT BAR**

This exotic relation to the vodka Gimlet became an instant classic when it was introduced at Summit Bar. The inspiration began with my love of shiso, which pairs nicely with the subtle spice of Vietnamese cinnamon agave, the sweetness of cucumber, and the tartness of lime juice. Combined with the smooth spices of the winter wheat of Russian Standard vodka and the candied pop of rhubarb bitters, it's a fresh take on a classic. Ladies and gentlemen, I'm pleased to introduce the Charmane Star!

FOUNDATION

SPIRIT	2 ounces Russian Standard vodka
SOUR	1 ounce fresh lime juice

DIMENSION

GARDEN	1 slice cucumber
HERB	1 whole shiso leaf
SWEET/SPICE	¾ ounce Vietnamese cinnamon agave mix (page 139)
BITTERS	1 dash rhubarb bitters

FINISH

HERB	1 smacked shiso leaf

METHOD

Muddle the cucumber and whole shiso leaf in a shaker tin. Add the vodka, lime juice, agave mix, and bitters and shake with ice. Double strain and pour over fresh ice. Garnish with the smacked shiso leaf.

GLASS	Double Old Fashioned
NOTABLE SUBSTITUTIONS	Aylesbury Duck (wheat vodka); Boyd & Blair

THE GUV'NOR

▸ SUMMIT BAR

My friend Gardner "Guv'nor" Dunn brought me into the world of Japanese whiskey. He's the ambassador for Suntory, the producer of Yamazaki whiskey. I have traveled the world over with this man (not always in one piece), so I figured the least I could do is name a drink after the old boy. Yamazaki is often seen as a "gateway" whiskey—creamier, rounder than scotch, with less smoke, and, in my opinion, perfect for mixing. At Summit, I use it in the Guv'nor. The pairing of Yamazaki with yuzu (an Asian fruit with a lime-orange-grapefruit flavor) along with fresh orange juice provides both an exotic floral tone and slight sweetness to the drink. This is balanced with the oaky mouthfeel of cardamom-infused agave and a finish of cardamom dust, creating a liquefied Zen garden in your glass.

ALCHEMIST NOTE

If you can't get hold of Yamazaki 12, you can come close to replicating its distinct flavor by using equal parts Bourbon and Scotch (use a Scotch that isn't very peaty). For those who don't care for whiskey, replacing it with vodka or gin and adding a dash of Angostura bitters makes for a tasty alternative, a variation known at Summit as the Governess.

FOUNDATION

SPIRIT	2 ounces Yamazaki 12-year-old Japanese whiskey
SOUR/EXOTIC	½ ounce unsalted yuzu juice

DIMENSION

SWEET/SPICE	¾ ounce cardamom-infused agave mix (page 137)
FRUIT	½ ounce fresh orange juice

FINISH

SPICE/AROMATIC	Ground cardamom

METHOD

Shake the whiskey, yuzu juice, agave mix, and orange juice with ice in a shaker tin. Double strain and pour over fresh ice. Sprinkle the top of the drink with cardamom.

GLASS	Large rocks or double Old Fashioned
NOTABLE SUBSTITUTIONS	A combination of equal parts Scotch (Glenrothes or Glenfiddich) and Bourbon (Eagle Rare 10-year-old or Michter's US*1 rye)

LIONS IN LONDON

▶ **SUMMIT BAR**

I fell in love with rooibos (a South African red bush tea) the first time I had a sip of it while on a safari in South Africa. It has a unique flavor, one that does not impart any of the tannic qualities of regular teas, a majestic mahogany color, outstanding flavor complexity, and a naturally sweet and floral finish with a slight nuttiness. Rooibos adds a harmonious new dimension to a Negroni-style cocktail. Infusing the clean flavor of Beefeater 24 in the tea and combining it with the rhubarb and orange notes of Aperol and the subtle floral notes of Dolin sweet vermouth make for a superb update on one of the great classics.

FOUNDATION

SPIRIT/TEA	1½ ounces rooibos-infused Beefeater gin (page 141)
SPIRIT	¾ ounce Aperol

DIMENSION

SWEET	½ ounce Dolin sweet vermouth
BITTERS	2 dashes Scrappy's orange bitters

FINISH

AROMATIC	Orange zest or orange peel

METHOD

Stir the gin, Aperol, vermouth, and bitters with ice in a mixing glass. Strain and serve over fresh ice. Garnish with orange zest.

GLASS	Rocks
NOTABLE SUBSTITUTIONS	Plymouth, Ford's, No. 3, Bombay Sapphire East

ALCHEMIST NOTE
Use Beefeater 24 for its brightness of grapefruit peel and the notes of Japanese sencha and green tea. The juniper is less dominant in this spirit, and the other botanicals are subtle enough to take on all the flavor of the rooibos tea without distracting from it.

SHE LOVES MEI, SHE LOVES MEI NOT

▶ **SUMMIT BAR**

My dear friend and travel partner Shauna Mei introduced me to her friend John Nevado, who has an organic edible rose farm in Ecuador. Pisco—a grape-based spirit—had been gaining popularity, and when the rose samples arrived, I thought they would add a striking component to a Pisco Sour. For my new little baby, I took agave and infused it with Szechuan peppercorn, which added a little buzz of citrus and pepper on the mouth, then finished with the floral notes of the edible rose petals floating atop a frothy egg-white sheen. As I added the rose petals, I thought about the child's game of pulling petals from a flower to see love is requited. "She loves me, she loves me not . . ." To be continued.

ALCHEMIST NOTE
Choosing the right pisco is an absolute must. Even at so-called Peruvian restaurants, I often see bartenders making Pisco Sours using pisco from Chile, which confuses the cocktail, as those are often aged in oak, making for a much fuller-bodied spirit. Peruvian pisco, on the other hand, is not aged, making it more about the grape flavor and a cleaner palate. Also, when looking for edible roses, look for organic—unsprayed—ones.

FOUNDATION

SPIRIT	2 ounces BarSol pisco
SOUR/EXOTIC	½ ounce unsalted yuzu juice

DIMENSION

FLORAL	2 edible rose petals, plus 2 for garnish (page 165)
TEXTURE	1 ounce egg white
SWEET/SPICE	¾ ounce Szechuan peppercorn–infused agave mix (page 139)

FINISH

BITTERS	1 dash Angostura bitters

METHOD

Muddle 2 of the rose petals in a shaker tin. Add the egg white and dry shake (without ice). Add the pisco and shake with ice. Double strain and pour over fresh ice. Garnish with the remaining rose petals.

GLASS	Large rocks or double Old Fashioned
NOTABLE SUBSTITUTIONS	Macchu Pisco, Pisco Portón

The three-spice, three-citrus botanicals of No. 3 are perfect for this cocktail. Its exotic citrus notes stay alive in the presence of the yuzu citrus and the spice of the shiso agave.

SUNRISE TO SUNDOWN

▶ NIKITA

The backdrop of the Pacific Ocean—the pristine beaches, soaring bluffs, and dramatic rock formations that seem like living creatures jutting out of the water—provided inspiration for the cocktails at Nikita, the bar I developed the cocktail program for in Malibu. ("Sunrise to Sundown" is an allusion to the hours posted on the signs of Malibu beaches.) This grand vista reminded me of my trips to Asia and the exotic flavors I encountered there. I combined gin, yuzu, and shiso leaf with a grapefruit finish, creating an exotic Tom Collins to welcome these flavors to this side of the Pacific.

FOUNDATION

SPIRIT	2 ounces No. 3 London Dry gin
SOUR/EXOTIC	½ ounce unsalted yuzu juice

DIMENSION

SWEET/HERB	¾ ounce shiso-infused agave mix (page 139)

FINISH

BITTERS/SOUR	2 dashes Scrappy's grapefruit bitters (page 165)
EFFERVESCENCE	1½ ounces club soda
AROMATIC	Grapefruit zest

METHOD

Shake the gin, yuzu juice, agave mix, and bitters with ice in a shaker tin. Add the club soda. Double strain and serve over fresh ice. Garnish with grapefruit zest.

GLASS	Collins or highball
NOTABLE SUBSTITUTIONS	Bombay Sapphire East, Plymouth, Ford's

THE COLONY

▶ NIKITA

While in Malibu, I felt it was apropos to make a cocktail that carried the opulent spirit of the area from the first sip to the last. My launching point was a popular cocktail from St. Tropez, La Piscina, a simple drink of Dom Pérignon with an ice cube. But being in SoCal, I began with an exploration of the California farmers' markets. I happened upon some of California's sweet, juicy strawberries, which I combined with elderflower and froze into ice cubes. Then I dropped the cube into a glass of Ruinart rosé, and voilà! As the ice cube melts in the glass, the detailed sweetness of the rosé shines through, transforming the drink with each sip. What can be more extravagant than a drink that keeps on giving?

ALCHEMIST NOTE

If Ruinart is in your budget, then by all means, enjoy. But any sparkling rosé that has nice berry notes and a creamy mouthfeel will work in this drink. Stay away from dryer wines, which will overpower the strawberry notes.

FOUNDATION

SPIRIT/ EFFERVESCENCE	5 ounces Ruinart Rosé

DIMENSION

FRUIT/AROMATIC	Strawberry elderflower ice cube (recipe follows)

FINISH

FLORAL	Viola or other edible flower (see recipe below)

METHOD

Put the strawberry elderflower ice cube in the glass. Pour the rosé over the ice cube. Allow to infuse for 2 minutes before serving.

GLASS	Coupe
NOTABLE SUBSTITUTIONS	Any sparkling rosé with bold berry notes

STRAWBERRY-ELDERFLOWER ICE CUBES ▸ MAKES 15 1-OUNCE CUBES

Fresh strawberries, pureed and strained to yield 12 ounces juice
(about 2- 2½ pints, depending on size of berries)

3 ounces elderflower syrup

15 violas or other edible flowers

Combine the strawberry juice with the elderflower syrup and pour into 1-inch silicone ice cube trays. Place one flower on top of each cube. Cover with plastic wrap and freeze.

Ice Mold

Spice

Sour

Garnish

Ladle

PUNCHES

PUNCHES ARE A FUN AND FESTIVE WAY TO INTRODUCE CRAFTED COCKTAILS
at a large gathering. The punch recipes in this section still use the Alchemist
principles for creating complex, layered flavor profiles, but have been adapted
for larger quantities. The end result: a quartet of deliciously balanced cocktail
punches.

The recipes in this section give instructions for making batches of 20 and
40 servings. (Note that a serving is one drink. Punch is popular, so adjust quantities according to how many servings you want, not how many guests you are
expecting.) I've given a suggested range of chilled water amounts to add to the
punch, which you can further adjust at the end to taste. Water replicates the
dilution you would get when you shake or stir an individual cocktail with ice.

In each of these recipes, I've suggested you make an ice mold, which is
basically a giant ice cube that will keep your punch chilled throughout the evening. Dilution from the ice mold melting over the course of the evening will also
affect the flavor and boldness of your punch, so keep that in mind when you add
the water.

PUNCH TIPS

+ A bowl that holds 4 to 8 quarts of liquid is a good size for just about any event. An 8-quart bowl will hold almost 80 servings.

+ The chilled filtered water proportions in these recipes are a guideline, but feel free to adjust them to taste, depending on how sweet (and potent) you want your punch to be.

+ Don't crowd the punch! Make sure the ice mold you make will fit comfortably in the punch bowl and isn't so large that guests won't be able to ladle out a drink.

MAKING ICE MOLDS

+ The recipes here call for freezing garnishes into an ice mold. This large block of ice not only keeps the punch chilled but adds a dramatic flair to the bottom of your punch bowl.

+ There are special containers you can buy to make ice molds in, which are available at any kitchen store. But you can also use any large Tupperware or other plastic container with a lid.

+ You may want to make extra ice molds so you can replace them as they melt.

+ To make the ice mold, fill the container about two thirds full with filtered water and drop in the garnishes. Put the lid on and freeze until it's solid.

+ To remove an ice mold from its container, tip the covered container upside down and run warm water over the bottom until you feel the ice mold slide loose.

BUONA VITA

The Buona Vita is a refreshing take on a classic Italian cocktail that I developed for the Luxury Collection that I then transformed into an elegant and refreshing sparkling punch. The mellow citrus notes of the Brooklyn gin, the subtle sweetness of the elderflower, the invigorating brightness of rhubarb notes in the Aperol and grapefruit, and the crisp bubbles of Prosecco will get any celebration off to a tasty start. Cheers to a life without worry.

ALCHEMIST NOTE
If you are planning on serving your punch in batches, remember to adjust the proportion of Prosecco and water as you go along.

SEIDER'S FORMULA

SERVING		20 SERVINGS	40 SERVINGS
FOUNDATION			
SPIRIT	Brooklyn gin	30 ounces	60 ounces
FLORAL/SWEET	St. Germain	20 ounces	40 ounces
FRUIT	Fresh ruby red grapefruit juice	30 ounces	60 ounces
DIMENSION			
SPIRIT/SWEET	Aperol	10 ounces	20 ounces
BITTERS	Scrappy's grapefruit bitters	½ ounce	1 ounce
FINISH			
EFFERVESCENCE	Prosecco	20 ounces	40 ounces
	Chilled filtered water	8 to 10 ounces	15 to 20 ounces
OPTIONAL	fresh berries	1 to 2 cups	2 to 4 cups
FOR THE ICE MOLDS	4 to 6 round lemon slices per mold		

METHOD

Make one or more ice molds with lemon slices (see page 125). In a large container with a lid, combine the gin, St. Germain, grapefruit juice, Aperol, and bitters. Cover and chill for at least 1 hour. About 20 minutes before serving, put the ice mold in the punch bowl, then add the chilled mixed ingredients. Top with Prosecco and add filtered water to taste. If using, add the berries to the punch bowl. Serve, replacing the ice mold if necessary.

NOTABLE SUBSTITUTIONS	No. 3 London Dry, Beefeater 24, Bombay Sapphire East

SEIDERHOUSE RUM PUNCH

Sipping on Hawaiian Punch as a kid was my nonalcoholic introduction to tiki drinks. This punch is my nod to the iconic class of tiki drinks. I stripped out the artificial flavors and replaced them with more modern ingredients. The tropical notes come from a New World Sauvignon Blanc. Vietnamese cinnamon brings a sweet, exotic spice. Diplomático rum doubles up on the sweetness and adds a rich, fruity kick. An aromatic dimension of Angostura and grapefruit brings a touch of citrus into the mix. I top this all off with a "punch" of color and dry fruit from a float of Pinot Noir.

SEIDER'S FORMULA

SERVING		20 SERVINGS	40 SERVINGS
FOUNDATION			
SPIRIT	Diplomático Reserva Exclusiva rum	20 ounces	40 ounces
SWEET/FLORAL	Dimmi Italian cordial	10 ounces	20 ounces
DIMENSION			
SWEET/SPICE	Vietnamese cinnamon agave mix (page 139)	15 ounces	30 ounces
BITTERS	Angostura bitters	¼ ounce	½ ounce
BITTERS	Scrappy's grapefruit bitters	¼ ounce	½ ounce
FINISH			
FRUIT	Pinot Noir	10 ounces	20 ounces
	Chilled filtered water	8 to 10 ounces	15 to 20 ounces
OPTIONAL	Cinnamon sticks for garnish		
FOR THE ICE MOLDS	5 to 7 cinnamon sticks per mold		

ALCHEMIST NOTE

For an additional bit of flair, omit the Pinot from the initial mix, and top each glass with a float (about ½ ounce) of the wine when serving.

METHOD

Make one or more ice molds with cinnamon sticks (see page 125). In a large container with a lid, combine the Sauvignon Blanc, rum, cordial, agave mix, bitters, and Pinot Noir. Cover and chill for at least 1 hour. About 20 minutes before serving, place the ice mold in the punch bowl, then add the chilled mixed ingredients. Add filtered water to taste. Add additional cinnamon sticks to the punch bowl, if desired. Serve, replacing the ice mold if necessary.

NOTABLE SUBSTITUTIONS	Blackwell, Zaya, Bacardi 8-year (rum); St. Germain, Cocchi Americano (cordial)

BOURBON HIBISCUS PUNCH

On a hot summer day, there are few things nicer than sipping on a Bourbon punch. This punch, born in Montauk on a Fourth of July weekend with friends, is an exotic southern Bourbon concoction that will raise the spirits of any celebration. The sweet, tangy hibiscus-infused agave, spicy candied ginger, honeysuckle notes in the Bourbon, and pop of ginger beer make for a combination as memorable as the holiday itself. Give me liberty or give me punch!

SEIDER'S FORMULA

SERVING		20 SERVINGS	40 SERVINGS
FOUNDATION			
SPIRIT	Jefferson Reserve Bourbon	40 ounces	80 ounces
SOUR	Fresh lemon juice	15 ounces	30 ounces
DIMENSION			
TEA/SWEET	Hibiscus-infused agave mix (page 138)	15 ounces	30 ounces
FINISH			
EFFERVESCENCE	Fever-Tree ginger beer	10 ounces	20 ounces
	Chilled filtered water	8 to 10 ounces	15 to 20 ounces
OPTIONAL	Lime wheels for garnish	5 to 7	8 to 10
FOR THE ICE MOLDS	About ½ cup dried hibiscus flowers per mold		

METHOD

Make one or more ice molds with hibiscus (see page 125). In a large container with a lid, combine the Bourbon, lemon juice, and agave mix. Cover and chill for at least 1 hour. About 20 minutes before serving, place the ice mold in the punch bowl, then add the chilled mixed ingredients. Top with the ginger beer and add filtered water to taste. Add the lime slices to the punch bowl, if desired. Serve, replacing the ice mold if necessary.

NOTABLE
SUBSTITUTIONS | Eagle Rare 10-year-old, Buffalo Trace

ALCHEMIST NOTE

If you want your punch to have more spicy notes than sweet ones, substitute rye for the Bourbon. And change the name of the drink!

THE LAST COCKTAIL

The Last Cocktail is a popular drink that can easily be adapted into a vibrant punch. The flavors work in every season, and it's a reliable crowd pleaser that you can bring out like a closing pitcher for any occasion. I particularly like to serve it at brunch, when the drink's distinctive combination of rosemary, pear nectar or puree, lemon, and Prosecco, accented by the subtle juniper-citrus notes of Spring 44, make for a surprising alternative to a Bellini or mimosa. I've found that even those who usually won't touch gin gravitate toward this celebratory concoction—one that leaves people talking long after they've seen the bottom of the punch bowl.

ALCHEMIST NOTE
Looza and R.W. Knudsen Family make pear nectars that are readily available in stores. Boiron and Perfect Purée brands have frozen purees you can order online.

SEIDER'S FORMULA

SERVING		20 SERVINGS	40 SERVINGS
FOUNDATION			
SPIRIT	Spring 44 gin	20 ounces	40 ounces
SOUR	Fresh lemon juice	20 ounces	40 ounces
DIMENSION			
SWEET/HERB	Rosemary-infused agave mix (page 139)	20 ounces	40 ounces
FRUIT	Pear puree or nectar	20 ounces	40 ounces
FINISH			
EFFERVESCENCE	Prosecco	20 ounces	40 ounces
	Chilled filtered water	8 to 10 ounces	15 to 20 ounces
OPTIONAL	Ground cloves for garnish		
FOR THE ICE MOLDS	About 7 rosemary sprigs per mold		

METHOD

Make one or more ice molds with rosemary sprigs (see page 125). In a large container with a lid, combine the gin, lemon juice, agave mix, and puree. Cover and chill for at least 1 hour. About 20 minutes before serving, place the ice mold in the punch bowl, then add the chilled mixed ingredients. Top with Prosecco and add filtered water to taste. Serve with a shaker of ground cloves for guests to sprinkle on top of each drinks with. Replace the ice mold if necessary.

NOTABLE SUBSTITUTIONS	Beefeater 24, No. 3 London Dry, Ford's

MIXES, INFUSIONS, BITTERS, PUREES, AND GARNISHES

AGAVE MIXES

I use organic light or amber agave nectar for my basic agave mix, which I use instead of simple syrup in my cocktails. Agave has a richer flavor than sugar, and a lower glycemic index, both of which improve the flavor and experience of drinking a cocktail. The unflavored mix can be infused with an infinite number of flavors; the recipes here are for the infusions called for in the recipes in this book, but feel free to experiment with other flavors. Here are a few general tips

▸ When making tea infusions, increase the amount of agave mix slightly because the tea will absorb some of the liquid.

▸ When making spice infusions, lightly toast the spices first to release their flavor. You'll know they are done when you see the first signs of smoke.

▸ Avoid pre-ground spices and powders, which will not have as fresh a flavor. Instead, use a coffee mill, spice grinder, or a mortar and pestle to grind whole spices. If you must use pre-ground spices, look for coarsely ground spices so they can be strained out.

▸ Each of these recipes makes about 750 ml (25 ounces). You can store your mixes in empty wine bottles, which makes them easy to pour out as you use them. Unless otherwise noted, all keep in the refrigerator for about two weeks.

AGAVE MIX:
Equal Parts Agave Nectar + Water

BLACK PEPPER-GINGER AGAVE MIX

25 ounces agave mix
1 (1-by-3-inch) piece fresh ginger, peeled and chopped
1 tablespoon coarsely ground black peppercorns

Put the agave mix and ginger in a blender and puree. Lightly toast the peppercorns in saucepan. Add the blended ginger mixture and bring to a light boil. Remove from heat, cover, and let stand for 30 minutes. Pour through a fine-mesh sieve, discard the solids, and transfer the mix to a clean bottle.

CARAWAY-INFUSED AGAVE MIX

¼ cup coarse ground cinnamon
25 ounces agave mix
4 tablespoons coarsely ground caraway seeds
25 ounces agave mix

Lightly toast the caraway in a sauce-pan. Add the agave mix and bring to a light boil. Remove from heat, cover, and let stand for 30 minutes. Pour through a fine-mesh sieve, discard the solids, and transfer the mix to a clean bottle.

CARDAMOM-INFUSED AGAVE MIX

¼ cup coarsely ground green cardamom pods
25 ounces agave mix

Lightly toast the cardamom in a saucepan. Add the agave mix and bring to a light boil. Remove from heat, cover, and let stand for 30 minutes. Pour through a fine-mesh sieve, discard the solids, and transfer the mix to a clean bottle.

CHIPOTLE CHILE AGAVE MIX

5 chipotle chiles, preferably morita type (they are deeper red)
25 ounces agave mix

Put the chiles and agave mix in a saucepan and bring to a light boil. Remove from heat, cover, and let stand for 30 minutes. Pour through a fine-mesh sieve and discard the solids. [Optional: For additional heat, preserve the softened chiles, seed them, and puree in a blender with the agave mix.] Transfer the mix to a clean bottle.

FENNEL-INFUSED AGAVE MIX

¼ cup coarsely ground fennel seeds
25 ounces agave mix

Lightly toast the fennel in a saucepan. Add the agave mix and bring to a light boil. Remove from heat, cover, and let stand for 30 minutes. Pour through a fine-mesh sieve, discard the solids, and transfer the mix to a clean bottle.

FIVE-SPICE AGAVE MIX

3 cinnamon sticks
2 teaspoons Szechuan peppercorns
½ tablespoon fennel seeds
1 teaspoon whole cloves
3 whole star anise
25 ounces agave mix

Coarsely grind the spices together in a spice grinder or with a mortar and pestle. Add the spice mixture to a saucepan and lightly toast. Add the agave mix and bring to a light boil. Remove from heat, cover, and let stand for 30 minutes. Pour through a fine-mesh sieve, discard the solids, and transfer the mix to a clean bottle.

HIBISCUS-INFUSED AGAVE MIX

¾ cup dried hibiscus (sometimes packaged as "hibiscus tea")
28 ounces agave mix

Combine the hibiscus and agave mix in a saucepan and bring to a light boil. Remove from heat, cover, and let stand for 30 minutes. Pour through a fine-mesh sieve, discard the solids, and transfer the mix to a clean bottle.

HOMEMADE GRENADINE SYRUP

13 ounces POM pomegranate juice
13 ounces light or amber agave nectar

Put the pomegranate juice and agave nectar in a clean bottle. Shake to combine.

LEMONGRASS PEPPERCORN AGAVE MIX

½ tablespoon coarsely ground black peppercorns
5 stalks lemongrass, chopped
25 ounces agave mix

Lightly toast the peppercorns in a saucepan. Add chopped lemongrass and agave mix and bring to light boil. Remove from heat, cover, and let stand for 30 minutes. Strain out lemongrass and black peppercorns and pour into a clean bottle.

MINT-AGAVE MIX

25 ounces agave mix
¾ cup packed fresh mint leaves (stems removed)

Put the agave mix and mint in a blender and puree. Let sit for 30 minutes. Pour through a fine-mesh sieve, discard the solids, and transfer the mix to a clean bottle. Note: covered and refrigerated, the mix will keep for just 3 days.

PINOT NOIR BLACK PEPPER AGAVE MIX

1 tablespoon coarsely ground black peppercorns
12½ ounces Pinot Noir wine
12½ ounces agave mix

Lightly toast the peppercorns in a saucepan. Add the wine and agave mix and bring to a light boil. Remove from heat, cover, and let stand for 30 minutes. Pour through a fine-mesh sieve, discard the solids, and transfer the mix to a clean bottle.

ROSEMARY-INFUSED AGAVE MIX

2 bunches fresh rosemary (about 20 sprigs)
25 ounces agave mix

Combine the rosemary agave mix in a saucepan and bring to a light boil. Remove from heat, cover, and let stand for 30 minutes. Pour through a fine-mesh sieve, discard the solids, and transfer the mix to a clean bottle.

SHISO-INFUSED AGAVE MIX

20 fresh shiso leaves (available at Japanese specialty stores)
25 ounces agave mix

Put the shiso and agave mix in a blender and puree. Let sit for 30 minutes. Pour through a fine-mesh sieve, discard the solids, and transfer the mix to a clean bottle. Note: covered and refrigerated, the mix will keep for just 3 days.

SZECHUAN PEPPERCORN-INFUSED AGAVE MIX

¼ cup coarsely ground Szechuan peppercorns
25 ounces agave mix

Lightly toast the Szechuan peppercorns in a saucepan. Add the agave mix and bring to a light boil. Remove from heat, cover, and let stand for 30 minutes. Pour through a fine-mesh sieve, discard the solids, and transfer the mix to a clean bottle.

VIETNAMESE CINNAMON AGAVE MIX

¼ cup coarsely ground Vietnamese (Saigon) cinnamon (available at specialty stores and online), or regular cinnamon
25 ounces agave mix

Lightly toast the cinnamon in a saucepan. Add the agave mix and bring to a light boil. Remove from heat, cover, and let stand for 30 minutes. Pour through a fine-mesh sieve, discard the solids, and transfer the mix to a clean bottle.

SPIRIT INFUSIONS

Spirit infusions last indefinitely in a closed bottle (you can store them in the same bottle the spirit came in), and like other spirits they do not need to be refrigerated. Don't be afraid to be bold and elevate that bottle of booze with one of these infusions.

CITRUS-INFUSED VODKA

Zest of 1 lemon, removed with a vegetable peeler
Zest of ½ orange, removed with a vegetable peeler
1 liter Russian Standard or other vodka

Shave off any white pith from the inside of the zests. Add the zests to the vodka. Cover, let stand for 3 days, then pour through a fine-mesh sieve and discard the solids. Return the vodka to the bottle and cover.

GEORGIA PEACH NECTAR ROOIBOS-INFUSED BOURBON

4 tablespoons Rare Tea Cellars Georgia Peach Nectar Rooibos tea
1 (750-ml) bottle Basil Hayden's or other Bourbon

Add the tea to the Bourbon. Cover, let stand for 2 hours, then pour through a fine-mesh sieve and discard the solids. Return the Bourbon to the bottle and cover.

GINGER ROOIBOS-INFUSED RYE

4 tablespoons Rare Tea Cellars ginger rooibos tea
1 (750-ml) bottle Mitcher's US*1 or other rye

Add the tea to the rye. Cover, let stand for 2 hours, then pour through a fine-mesh sieve and discard the solids. Return the rye to the bottle and cover.

HONEYBUSH-INFUSED SCOTCH

4 tablespoons loose-leaf honeybush tea
1 (750-ml) bottle blended Scotch (I use Glenrothes Select or Famous Grouse)

Add the tea to the Scotch. Cover, let stand for 2 hours, then pour through a fine-mesh sieve and discard the solids. Return the Scotch to the bottle and cover.

RAISIN-INFUSED RYE

1 cup sultana raisins
1 (750-ml) bottle rye

In a glass jar or other nonreactive container, combine the raisins and rye. Cover, let stand for 4 to 5 days, then pour through a fine-mesh sieve. Reserve the soaked raisins for garnishing (see page 145). Return the rye to its bottle and cover.

ROOIBOS-INFUSED GIN

4 tablespoons loose-leaf rooibos tea
1 (750-ml) bottle Beefeater 24 gin

Add the tea to the gin. Cover, let stand for 2 hours, then pour through a fine-mesh sieve and discard the solids. Return the gin to the bottle and cover.

TOASTED COCONUT-INFUSED RUM

¾ cup unsweetened shredded coconut
12½ ounces Caña Brava rum
12½ ounces Flor de Cana 7-year rum

Toast the coconut in a 250°F oven until golden brown, about 15 to 20 minutes. Let cool. In a glass jar or other nonreactive container, combine the coconut and rums. Cover, let stand for 3 to 4 days, then pour through a fine-mesh sieve and discard the solids. Transfer the rum to a clean bottle and cover.

BITTERS AND TINCTURES

Bitters and tinctures add complexity and dimension to your cocktails. They act as synergists, highlighting and binding the flavors of spirits and other ingredients together. The difference between bitters and tinctures is that bitters have a bittering ingredient (a root or a bark) while tinctures do not. Experiment with them in Alchemist drinks, or use them as a flavor elevation in classic drinks like a vodka on the rocks or a Gin and Tonic.

▸ Old-fashioned restaurant oil and vinegar bottles are perfect and inexpensive vessels with which to dispense bitters and tinctures.

▸ Use the highest proof, neutral spirit you can find to make your bitters and tinctures—ideally 140 or higher. The higher the proof, the more flavor will be extracted from the ingredients. Try Everclear, Devil's Springs, or any unflavored vodka that's at least 100 proof.

▸ All recipes make 10 ounces, and will keep indefinitely.

CINNAMON BITTERS

10 ounces high-proof alcohol

1 tablespoon coarsely ground smoked cinnamon (available at specialty spice purveyors; see page 165)

Combine the alcohol and cinnamon in a glass jar or other nonreactive container. Cover and let sit at room temperature for 5 to 7 days, then pour through a fine-mesh sieve and discard the solids. Transfer the tincture to a clean bottle and cover.

SARSAPARILLA BITTERS

10 ounces high-proof alcohol

4 tablespoons sarsaparilla bark (see page 165)

2 tablespoons sassafras bark (see page 165)

Combine all the ingredients in a glass jar or other nonreactive container. Cover and let sit at room temperature for 5 to 7 days, then pour through a fine-mesh sieve and discard the solids. Transfer the bitters to a clean bottle and cover.

SPICED CRANBERRY BITTERS

10 ounces high-proof alcohol

¾ cup dried cranberries

½ cinnamon stick

Combine all the ingredients in a glass jar or other nonreactive container. Cover and let sit at room temperature for 5 to 7 days, then pour through a fine-mesh sieve and discard the solids. Transfer the bitters to a clean bottle and cover.

CHIPOTLE TINCTURE

10 ounces high-proof alcohol

3 dried chipotle chiles, preferably morita type (they are deeper red)

Combine the alcohol and chiles in a glass jar or other nonreactive container. Cover and let sit at room temperature for 4 to 5 days, then pour through a fine-mesh sieve and discard the solids. Transfer the tincture to a clean bottle and cover.

KAFFIR LIME TINCTURE

10 ounces high-proof alcohol
20 fresh kaffir lime leaves

Combine the alcohol and kaffir lime leaves in a glass jar or other nonreactive container. Cover and let sit at room temperature for 5 to 7 days, then pour through a fine-mesh sieve and discard the solids. Transfer the tincture to a clean bottle and cover.

LEMONGRASS-PEPPERCORN TINCTURE

10 ounces high-proof alcohol
4 lemongrass stalks, chopped
1 teaspoon coarsely ground black peppercorns

Combine all the ingredients in a glass jar or other nonreactive container. Cover and let sit at room temperature for 5 to 7 days, then pour through a fine-mesh sieve and discard the solids. Transfer the tincture to a clean bottle and cover.

ROOIBOS TINCTURE

10 ounces high-proof alcohol
1½ tablespoons loose-leaf rooibos tea

Combine the alcohol and tea in a glass jar or other nonreactive container. Cover and let sit at room temperature for 3 days, then pour through a fine-mesh sieve and discard the solids. Transfer the tincture to a clean bottle and cover.

SAFFRON TINCTURE

10 ounces high-proof alcohol
½ ounce (1 - 1½ grams) saffron threads
1 orange peel, removed with a vegetable peeler

Combine the alcohol and saffron in a saucepan. Place over low heat just until the saffron blooms, turning the alcohol a rich orange color. Put the orange peel in a glass jar or other nonreactive container and pour the saffron alcohol over it. Let cool, cover, and let sit at room temperature for 1 day. Fish out and discard the orange peel. Let the tincture infuse for 5 to 7 more days. Transfer to a clean bottle and cover.

GARNISHES

BOURBON-SOAKED APRICOTS

1 cup dried apricots
4 ounces Bourbon

Combine the apricots and Bourbon in a glass jar or other nonreactive container. Cover and let sit at room temperature for at least 3 days. (You may leave the apricots in the Bourbon indefinitely.)

BOURBON- OR MADEIRA-SOAKED CHERRIES

1 cup drained Luxardo marasca cherries
4 ounces Bourbon or Madeira wine

Combine the cherries and wine in a glass jar or other nonreactive container. Cover and let sit at room temperature for at least 3 days. (You may leave the cherries in spirit indefinitely.)

RYE-SOAKED RAISINS

1 cup raisins
4 ounces rye

Combine the raisins and rye in a glass jar or other nonreactive container. Cover and let sit at room temperature for at least 3 days. (You may leave the raisins in the rye indefinitely.) Alternatively, you can make a batch of raisin-infused rye (page 141) and use those raisins as a garnish.

KAFFIR LIME SALT

1 (8 ½-ounce) box Maldon sea salt
1 tablespoon kaffir lime powder (see page 165)

Combine the salt and kaffir lime powder in a glass jar and cover. The salt will keep indefinitely.

PUREES

CINNAMON PINEAPPLE PUREE

MAKES 750 ML / 25 OUNCES

4 cups chopped fresh pineapple
2 ounces pineapple juice
12 ounces Vietnamese cinnamon agave (page 139)

Put all the ingredients in a blender and puree. (You may want to add the pineapple in stages.) Pour into a clean bottle. Refrigerated and covered, the puree will keep for 1 week.

JALAPEÑO PINEAPPLE PUREE

MAKES 750 ML / 25 OUNCES

1 medium pineapple, peeled, cored, and chopped (about 5 cups)
4 ounces pineapple juice
1 jalapeño chile, roughly chopped

Put all the ingredients in a blender and puree. (You may want to add the pineapple in stages.) Pour into a clean bottle. Refrigerated and covered, the puree will keep for 5 days.

PEAR ROSEMARY PUREE

MAKES 750 ML / 25 OUNCES

20 ounces Boiron pear puree (or Looza or R.W. Knudsen Family pear nectar)
5 ounces rosemary-infused agave mix (page 139)

Combine the pear puree and agave mix in blender. Pour into a clean bottle. Refrigerated and covered, the puree will keep for 1 week.

RED PEPPER PUREE

MAKES 20 OUNCES

5 red bell peppers, seeded and chopped
2 ounces water

Put the peppers and water in a blender and puree. (You may want to add the peppers in stages.) Pour into a clean bottle. Refrigerated and covered, the puree will keep for 2 days.

TOOLS
AND
TECHNIQUES

TOOLS

ATOMIZER: Atomizers are great for adding an aromatic layer or finish to your cocktails. Misting the inside of the glass with an atomizer is a great alternative to the traditional absinthe "rinse" used in the preparation of the Sazerac and the Shu Jam Fizz. (1)

BAR SPOONS: I use two different types of bar spoons. For stirring drinks, I use a Japanese spoon that is very long, so I have a bigger range of motion when I stir. For cracking ice, I use a disk spoon, which has a wider mouth. (2)

JIGGERS: These are essential tools to ensure you get exact amounts in each drink. Some of the recipes in this book call for quantities of as little as ¼ ounce, and eyeballing them can mess up the precise balance of flavors my drinks call for. Would you bake a cake without using measuring spoons? It's just not gonna taste right, kids!

The ideal jigger indicates measurements from ¼ ounce to 2 ounces. The important thing is that the measurements are clearly marked, and you like how the jigger feels in your hand, as ease of use is also an essential part of making a great drink. (3)

MICROPLANE GRATER: Essential for zesting fruit and garnishes. (4)

MIXING GLASS: My favorite mixing glass is the Japanese Yarai. Not only is it visually stunning, but it also works better than a pint glass, which is traditionally used for mixing drinks. The Yarai has a wider base, which allows you to stir a cocktail quickly, without fear of tipping the drink over. It also holds more ice than a pint glass, which lets you chill a drink to the proper temperature and achieve the right amount of dilution more quickly. The addition of a lip helps prevent spillage when pouring. Another advantage is that the Yarai comes in multiple sizes; the largest size is big enough to mix two complete drinks at the same time. (5)

MUDDLER: A muddler is used to crush herbs, citrus, fruit, and garden ingredients. Muddlers can be made either from wood or plastic (the plastic ones are more durable). When using a muddler, you want to gently smash the ingredients, without bruising or pulverizing them into little pieces. (6)

peels for twists and garnishes. I like ceramic peelers because they stay sharp and don't rust. When you peel citrus, peel from top to bottom of the fruit so that you get a section of peel with enough structure to allow you to squeeze out the oils. (7)

SHAKER TIN: For shaken drinks, I use an 18-ounce metal shaker (8) and a 28-ounce metal shaker (9) together, rather than a cobbler shaker or single shaker with a lid. With cobbler shakers, the lid often gets stuck on top after the shake; by using two tins in the sizes above, you'll get a good shake, and still be able to remove the top tin easily. I prefer tin shakers because they are lighter and conduct temperature quicker than the traditional Boston shaker, which is made of glass.

SPICE SHAKER: For dispensing

ground spices. Use spice shakers, rather than regular salt and pepper shakers, because their wider mouth ensures a more even dispensing of powder.

STRAINERS: There are three basic types of strainers:

HAWTHORNE STRAINER: This is the most versatile strainer, and if you are only going to buy one, this is the one to get. A Hawthorne strainer is used as the top (first) strainer in shaken drinks, and is placed over the large shaker tin. It's worth it to buy a good-quality one because the coil will last longer. With lesser versions, the coil unwinds after use and the strainer won't fit snugly over the shaker tin. (10)

TEA STRAINER: An essential tool for the advanced mixologist, a mesh tea strainer is used as the second strainer in shaken drinks (hence the phrase "double strain"). It is held directly on top of the glass and is used to finely strain out unwanted fragments of ingredients or shards of ice that will muddle the flavor of the drink. You can also buy special mesh cocktail strainers, which serve the same purpose. (11)

JULEP: A julep is recommended for stirred drinks. It doesn't have coils, so it fits better on top of the ice that should poke over the mixing glass. Note: Only shaken drinks are typically double-strained, so this is the only strainer you need for stirred drinks. (12)

CONSTRUCTING the COCKTAIL

KNOW THE SEQUENCE: I teach my bartenders to build their drinks using a specific order: Bitters, Sweet, Sour, Spirit, Ice. This ensures that you spare the most expensive ingredient (spirit) from any missteps along the way. Adding ice last keeps your cocktail from getting overly diluted by limiting the amount of time your ingredients are in the ice, which gives you more control over the final result.

BUILD THE INGREDIENTS: With the exception of dashes of bitters or tinctures (which are added directly into the mixing glass or shaker tin), measure ingredients with the jigger, being sure to keep it level, as even a slight tilt will lead to an inaccurate measurement. Keep it close to the rim so you can pour without spilling.

PAY ATTENTION TO THE ICE: Having the right amount of ice is essential, as temperature and dilution are crucial to the balance and taste of drinks. For shaken drinks, that means filling the large shaker tin at least three quarters full of ice. For stirred drinks, add ice (a combination of full cubes and cracked ones) until the ice is above the liquid line. (This may mean that the ice goes above the rim of a glass, which is why a julep strainer comes in handy.)

Use ice cubes that are at least 1-inch square, as smaller cubes will melt faster and dilute a drink too much. Ideally, you want 1-inch cubes for tall drinks and 2-inch cubes for short drinks. Whenever possible, use filtered water to make your ice.

If you are fanatical about getting your ice crystal clear, you can make your own cubes out of a large ice mold. To do this, let the water sit out for at least an hour before you freeze it, which will let some of the impurities evaporate. Then freeze it in a large uncovered container, which lets the ice freeze more slowly, letting the remaining impurities settle at the bottom. When it's frozen, chip off the unclear section at the bottom and chip out large, clear cubes from the rest of the block.

STRAIN PROPERLY: After you've shaken or stirred the ingredients, strain your cocktail into the glass quickly, with the mixing glass or shaker tin elevated above the glass, to create more aeration, which gives a frothy texture. "Double strain" means to strain a shaken drink with both a Hawthorne strainer placed on the shaker tin and a tea strainer placed on the actual glass, to remove ice shards and fragments of ingredients which can upset the balance of flavors. Stirred drinks need to be strained only once, using a julep strainer if possible.

FINISHING/GARNISHING:

There are several specific techniques for finishing and garnishing drinks. Most are about releasing oils and the essence of citrus, spices, or herbs, which create the aromatic quality that makes up the finish of many cocktails.

ATOMIZING AND DUSTING: When using an atomizer or dusting spices, spray or sprinkle from a slight distance, so you get an even coverage on top of the cocktail.

SMACKING: Place a few leaves of whatever herb you are smacking in one palm and give them a light, open-handed smack with the other hand. Don't hit the leaves so hard that they tear, as you don't want to end up with shreds of leaf in the drink.

TWISTING: Pinch the citrus peel parallel to the glass, level to the rim, so that the oils fall softly into the completed drink. Do not twist directly over the cocktail, as this will overwhelm the balance of the drink with excess citrus oils. Use this technique whenever a recipe calls for a garnish of citrus peel, giving the peel a pinch first before you twist it inside the glass.

ZESTING: Grated zest is typically used as a garnish on shaken drinks with a citrus component (such as lemon or lime juice) so you experience the mouthfeel of the zest when it sits on the froth that the shaking creates. (In a stirred drink, the zest would fall to the bottom.) When zesting citrus, grate with the fruit underneath the Microplane, so you can see how much zest you are creating before it goes into the drink. When you have the right amount of zest (eyeball about a teaspoon per drink), turn the grater over and tap it into the drink so zest falls in all at once and disperses. While zesting, rotate the fruit continually so as not to grate into the bitter, white part.

SHAKING COCKTAILS

WHEN PREPARING A SHAKEN DRINK, FILL THE LARGER SHAKER TIN AT LEAST three quarters of the way full with ice so that the liquid has plenty of ice to pass through. (Only use full cubes of ice in shaken drinks, never cracked ice.) This will allow the drink to chill quickly and achieve the right amount of dilution. After you fill the large shaker with ice, add ingredients to the small shaker and seal the two tins so the small shaker is on top.

HARD SHAKE: This is the shake you'll use for most cocktails, and all of the cocktails in this book, unless otherwise specified. A hard shake is a vigorous shake, continuing for about eight seconds. You want to keep the shaker moving in a vertical motion, from your shoulders to your hips, rather than swishing it back and forth. This will let you use gravity to help get the cocktail properly mixed. Keep your elbows by your sides, and pivot within a 90-degree range of motion to ensure the ice is traveling back and forth from the top of the small shaker to the bottom of the large one. To gauge if the drink is the right temperature, grip the bottom of large shaker and top of the small shaker. You'll know your cocktail is ready when you feel as if you just made a snowball with your bare hands.

SHORT SHAKE: A short shake is done with the same vigorousness as a hard shake, but for about half the time (about four seconds). This is used when making cocktails such as a French 75 that have an effervescent ingredient added at the end. Because those ingredients add additional dilution, the rest of the ingredients don't need as much contact with the ice.

ROLL SHAKE: This is a very gentle alternative to a regular shake, where you roll your wrist back and forth a couple of times just to add some aeration and texture to a drink right before it is served. You use it when you want to mix ingredients without adding additional dilution. I use it for drinks such as a Dark and Stormy: The roll shake will mix the cocktail just enough, without irritating the carbonation of the ginger beer.

To pour the shaken drink, place the Hawthorne strainer over the large shaker, and hold the tea strainer over the glass. If your drink is served on the rocks, fill it to the rim with ice. Make sure you use new ("fresh") ice in the glass, rather than recycling the ice from the shaker tin.

Middle of Shake

Top of Shake

Bottom of Shake

STIRRING COCKTAILS

IF A DRINK DOES NOT HAVE CITRUS IN THE FOUNDATION, IT WILL USUALLY BE stirred. The point of stirring is to achieve a silky and viscous mouthfeel, devoid of any air bubbles, ice shards, or fragments of ingredients (though some people prefer their Martinis shaken because they like the ice shards that chip off in the process).

The particulars of this technique are important. If possible, use a thick mixing glass made of thick glass (such as the Japanese Yarai) that holds a good amount of ice. (As an alternative, you can use the large tin of a large metal shaker.) After you add the ingredients to the mixing glass, crack a few cubes with a bar spoon and add those with solid cubes to the mixing glass. The cracked cubes combine with the solid cubes to form a base, like grout between a layer of bricks. This will ensure that the ice is submerged below the liquid line, which will help your drink to chill properly.

▶ To crack ice, hold a cube in the palm of your hand so a flat side is upright. In one motion, give it a quick smack with the back of a wide bar spoon. Don't worry, it's not gonna hurt if you miss.

▶ Always stir clockwise, rotating the spoon inside the mixing glass. The stem of the spoon will push ice ahead so liquid and ice rotate gracefully.

TWO-PART STIRRING TECHNIQUE

Hold the spoon between your thumb and index finger, with the middle finger on the outside of the glass. Pull the spoon clockwise with middle finger from 12' o'clock to 6 o'clock.

Push the shaft of the spoon with the ring finger around the rest of mixing glass from 6 o'clock to 12 o'clock. Stir each drink briskly, about 50 times, to ensure that the cocktail is properly chilled. Pour it in the serving glass using a julep strainer.

SEIDER'S CHOSEN ONES . . .

THESE ARE THE SPIRITS I PERSONALLY CONSUME AND MIX MY COCKTAILS WITH, chosen on their merits. (I try not to let my sensitive palate be swayed by bonuses or trips to far-off lands . . . although if someone is willing to buy a few hundred copies of this book, I may reconsider.) They stand here before you because they've been made with good-quality ingredients and superior craftsmanship. Investing in one or more of these will give your cocktails a starting point of success before you shake or stir.

Make sure you try each spirit on its own before mixing it with others. Tasting spirits straight beforehand will train your palate to pick out each one's unique flavor profile, which will in turn help you to determine what other ingredients to add to each one to make a great cocktail, or elevate certain classics. A Tom Collins made with No. 3 gin tastes completely different from one made with Beefeater. A Rittenhouse Old Fashioned is a different drink from one made with Knob Creek rye.

I remember one day I wanted to find out what gin made the best Gin and Tonic. I went through every gin in my joint before coming to my conclusion. (My choice is a secret, but ply me with a couple of shots and I might let you in on it.) I've done this with whiskeys (for Old Fashioneds), tequilas (for Margaritas), and whenever I develop a new Alchemist creation. Of course, I work in a bar, and if you have a friend with a bad-ass liquor cabinet or an unlimited expense account, have at it. But even if you don't have access to a bar, the point is that the better you understand the taste of the spirits themselves, the better your finished cocktails will taste. With my recommended spirits as your guide, start fine-tuning your ability to detect the different nuances of flavor among gins, whiskeys, tequilas, and vodkas. The service any of these spirits provides in a cocktail will be first-class, so just be sure you don't crash the plane by ignoring their particular flavors and characteristics.

VODKA

WHEAT VODKA

AYLESBURY DUCK: This vodka is made from winter wheat from the western Rockies of Canada, which gives it a spicy and rich grain flavor. It's a great pick when you want a vodka with a combination of creamy mouthfeel and spirit presence, such as in a variation on a Gimlet or in a Vodka Tonic.

RUSSIAN STANDARD: I wanted to use only one brand of vodka when we opened up Summit Bar, and this is the one I chose. Russian Standard is made from winter wheat from the Russian black steppes and water from Lake Ladoga. The power and spice of this wheat add a nice depth and presence to mixed drinks. It also has a nice clean finish that doesn't jeopardize delicate ingredients, such as the shiso leaf in the Charmane Star.

RUSSIAN STANDARD PLATINUM: This is Russian Standard's higher-end vodka. It's great if you want an ultra-crisp, ultra-smooth vodka. It has a creamy, rich mouthfeel that is really pleasing to the palate. I enjoy sipping this on the rocks with a dash of orange bitters.

ZU BISON GRASS VODKA: My good friend Daniel "the Hammer" Undhammar, who is the brand ambassador for ZU Bison, reintroduced me to this uniquely flavored vodka. The ZU stands for Zubrowka ("bison" in Polish), and it comes from the northeast of Poland, in the last primeval forest, Bialowieza, where these bison can be found. The bison grass gives it a distinct flavor, which makes for a great twist in a Vodka Tonic or a Moscow Mule. It is rich and creamy in the mouth and has a slightly spicy vanilla flavor with a touch of pistachio and citrus notes. I love to mix it with apple juice and hard cider.

POTATO VODKA

Potato vodkas are not as lean, and are richer on the mouth than wheat vodkas. (They are also naturally gluten-free.) They are great choices for any classic-style drink.

BOYD & BLAIR: The Pennsylvania potatoes in this vodka add a distinct savory flavor, which is combined with its exceptionally smooth, creamy finish. It goes great with a touch of celery bitters or in a variation on a Martini with a rinse of caraway aquavit.

KARLSSON'S GOLD: This vodka is made from a blend of seven different types of Swedish potatoes. It's great on the rocks with a sprinkle of cracked black pepper.

GIN

NEW AMERICAN/NEW WESTERN

This category of gins contains spirits with two different flavor profiles: aromatic (gins which have complex spice and citrus notes, and soft juniper and pine) and gins that are evenly balanced between citrus and pine.

BEEFEATER 24: The "24" in this variety of Beefeater gin stands for the twenty-four-hour steeping process each batch undergoes. The signature twelve-botanical blend includes hand-prepped grapefruit and Seville oranges, and the aromatics of Japanese and Chinese teas. Because of these citrus and tea notes, I often use it to make tea infusions.

BOMBAY SAPPHIRE EAST: Most gin producers steep or macerate botanicals in a neutral spirit before distilling. Bombay uses a botanical basket hung in the still, through which vapors from the distilled neutral spirit must pass during the distillation process. The resulting flavors are soft, and not at all overbearing. East has all the botanicals of traditional Bombay Sapphire, with the addition of lemongrass and black peppercorn. It works particularly well in cocktails with Asian flavors like lemongrass and Thai basil.

BROOKLYN GIN: Created by my two good friends, Joe and Emil. They peel, cut, and crack all of the citrus and juniper that go into their gin by hand. This vibrant spirit is useful when you want to add a complex citrus element to a cocktail on top of regular lemon or lime juice.

CADENHEAD'S OLD RAJ: Old Raj is infused with saffron, in addition to juniper, citrus, nuts, and spices. Because it's 110 proof, it has a strong backbone that holds up drink with a number of ingredients in it, such as the Apology.

FORD'S: Ford's gin has a backbone of juniper and coriander seed that's balanced with citrus (bitter orange, lemon, and grapefruit peels), floral (jasmine flower and orris root), and spice (angelica and cassia). I use Ford's in classic drinks as a fresher, more complex alternative to the traditional juniper-forward UK-style gins. The three citrus elements give a bright pop in the mid-palate that adds a nice dimension to a traditional Gin and Tonic or a Gimlet, as well as in more complex Alchemist recipes.

NO. 3 LONDON DRY: No. 3 gets its name from No. 3 St. James Street in London, the historic home of the Berry Bros. & Rudd, one of England's oldest spirit purveyors. This gin contains a blend of three spices (angelica, coriander, and cardamom) and three fruit notes (Spanish orange, grapefruit, and juniper). The initial whoosh of juniper is balanced by a brightness of citrus and spice that stay alive in the exotic flavors I use in many of my Alchemist cocktails. It's also great in more straightforward gin drinks, like Martinis and Gin and Tonics

SPRING 44: The Spring 44 guys source their water from a remote area in the northern Colorado Rocky Mountains (at the elevation of 9,044 feet). The water up there is some of the smoothest and cleanest I have ever tasted. In addition to the juniper and floral notes, there is mint, lavender, and even rosemary in the mix. It is a versatile gin that you can sip or mix. The company also has a barrel-aged Old Tom gin (a gin that's been aged in Bourbon barrels) that makes for a great twist on a Tom Collins.

LONDON DRY

The style of gin with the most piney juniper flavor.

BEEFEATER: Beefeater London Dry gin is one of the oldest modern gins, and it's the only gin currently produced in London. It is juniper-forward and smooth, but has a complexity from its eight-botanical blend that other London Dry gins don't. This is my favorite London Dry style for classic gin cocktails.

PLYMOUTH: Plymouth gin is a category by itself. It is made on the sixteenth-century Dominican Friary where the Pilgrims stayed the night before they set out for America. It has a clean flavor with a touch of sweetness and notes of pine, citrus, and black pepper. It is useful in cocktails where you want to introduce a slight touch of botanicals.

BOURBON/RYE

BASIL HAYDEN'S: White pepper, oak, and vanilla aromas combine with warm honey, soft caramel, and orange marmalade in this spirit. This combination helps synergize drinks that have both citrus and warm spice, without adding too much boozy heat.

BUFFALO TRACE: Buffalo Trace is another quality Bourbon at a great price. It is 90 proof, so has enough power to hold its own in a bold cocktail like the John Lee Hooker. Its finish is very mellow, smooth but with the right amount of alcohol bite.

EAGLE RARE 10-YEAR-OLD: This is a single-barrel Bourbon, so each batch has its own individual personality. Eagle Rare 10 has a cleaner fruit and spice compo-nent than many other bourbons and is also not as oak dominant, with a long, lingering finish. It is a little more expensive than Rittenhouse, but for the money, you can't get a better sipping or mixing Bourbon. If you can find the 17-year-old, you are in for a special treat.

JEFFERSON'S RESERVE: The first Bourbon released by Jefferson's, the Reserve is a complex yet balanced combination of three different Bourbons, including a whiskey aged up to twenty years in American oak. The result is a medium-weight Bourbon with a dry, robust palate that fills the mouth with flavors of roasted corn, caramel, toffee, and oak. This is a great choice for sipping or when you want to add complexity to any stirred cocktail. Their 18-year Presidential selection is a must-sip Bourbon as well.

KNOB CREEK: Booker Noe started the small-batch Bourbon movement, and among his creations is Knob Creek rye (named for small stream that flowed through President's Abraham Lincoln's childhood home in Kentucky). Knob Creek has a vibrant and spicy mouthfeel, with cin-namon, mint, charcoal, honeyed fruit, and caramel. This is one of my favorite ryes to use in cocktails, because the flavor profile adds a profound depth to any drink it's used with.

MITCHER'S US*1 STRAIGHT: Known as the "whiskey that warmed the American Revolution," Mitcher's was established in 1753 and was the first commercial distillery in America. This distillery's rye is sheared from its outer husk, which creates more flavor during fermentation. It has hints of black pepper, baked spice, and marmalade, all of which are balanced by herbal notes. It is a great choice for sipping, and also when you want a rye that will add a rich mouthfeel to a cocktail.

RITTENHOUSE: For mixing spirits, Rittenhouse rye is one of the best values in terms of quality for the money. It has a dark cherry nose, with vanilla, caramel, and spice that come out along the palate, and a long, citrusy finish. It's "bottled in bond," which means that all bottles are the product of a single distillery, made in a single season, in a single year, which ensures a consistency of flavor. At 100 proof, it has enough of a backbone to stand out in mixed drinks, but still feels like a rich spirit with nice nuances of spices and aromatics of rye bread, which was why I paired it with raisins in the Situation.

OVERPROOF WHISKEYS

These selections add an ethereal flavor profile to stirred cocktails such as the classic Old Fashioned. The slight dilution of stirring rounds the high-proof heat and brings out certain flavors you won't get in lower-proof alternatives.

BAKER'S 107: The caramel-vanilla mouthfeel and fruit/nut/spice flavors of this higher-proof Baker's whiskey blend perfectly in a Manhattan-style drink.

KNOB CREEK SINGLE BARREL RESERVE: Each barrel of this 120-proof rye is bottled individually, and thus will have its own unique variations in taste, color, and aroma. Overall, it's smooth and complex, with the overproof backbone that holds up in any Alchemist drink. It can also be used as a bigger-spirit alternative to regular whiskey in a classic like the Manhattan.

JAPANESE WHISKEY

YAMAZAKI 12-YEAR-OLD: I have a special fondness for the Suntory family, who make Yamazaki Japanese whiskey: Gardner "Guv" Dunn, Satoru Shimizu, Yoshi Morimoto, Neyah White, and Mike Miyamoto. They brought me to their country and really showed me a magical time in Japan. (Arigato!) The Yamazaki distilleries are surrounded by incredible temples, exotic forests, and incredibly pristine water. In fact, the distillers searched all over Japan before selecting Mount Kaikomagatake as the source of their water. The water gives a beautiful richness of mouthfeel that balances with the winter spice and sweetness of tropical fruit notes, which is what sets this spirit on another level for me. Yamazaki was the catalyst for one of my most famous cocktails, the Guv'nor. I also like Suntory's **Hakushu** whiskey, which has brighter, fresher notes.

TEQUILA AND MEZCAL

CABEZA BLANCO: Cabeza is produced from estate-owned agave plants that are hand-picked at their ideal ripening point (seven to nine years), which is older than the agave used in many tequilas. Cabeza is also higher in proof, which helps its bright green pepper and agave flavors to maintain their presence in Margarita-style drinks.

DON AMADO BLANCO OR REPOSADO: Don Amado has been producing some of the best mezcal in Oaxaca for eleven generations, and, like Cabeza, this mezcal is produced from only estate-owned agave, which allows its producers to control for brighter sugar levels in the spirit. I had the pleasure of visiting the their distillery with owner Jacob Lustig and saw the love and attention put into each bottle. The mezcal has a well-balanced smokiness with citrus and floral notes. It highlights the spice and aromatics and adds just the right level of smoke to some of my more exotic and delicate creations.

ILEGAL REPOSADO: Ilegal is made in Tlacolula, Oaxaca, by a fourth-generation *mezcalero* and his family. Using five-hundred-year-old methods, they craft a mezcal rich in agave flavor and lightly accented with smoke. Ilegal is aged for four months in a combination of new oak and re-charred whiskey barrels. The fruit of the agave is very present, accompanied by notes of butterscotch, caramelized pear, and tobacco, with a subtle fade of smoke on the finish. It isn't cheap, but if you have the money, the depth of flavor in Ilegal is a unique taste you can't find in less-expensive brands.

OLMECOS ALTOS: This tequila has fresh herbal notes, complemented by green pepper and a touch of citrus finish. On the mouth, it has a sweet and slightly smoky feel, balanced by bright, vegetal flavors with a final soft honey flavor. It adds complexity to tequila-based cocktails that doesn't get drowned out by the citrus juice.

RUM

BANKS 5 ISLAND: Created by my friend Jim Meehan and named after the eighteenth-century English naturalist Sir Joseph Banks, this intriguing rum is composed of five different rums from distilleries located on the islands of Jamaica, Trinidad, Barbados, Guyana, and Indonesia. It has a very complex finish with a cool funk from the unique blend of rums of different ages. It has a surprising vegetal brightness that adds to the overall uniqueness of this spirit. If you find yourself in a Daiquiri-making contest, Banks will deliver the prize every time.

CAÑA BRAVA BLANCO: Francisco "Don Pancho" J. Fernandez, the master distiller at Las Cabres, made rum in his native Cuba for more than thirty-five years before moving to this Panamanian distillery where Caña Brava is produced. His expertise makes this spirit taste exactly like Cuban rum should: fresh-pressed sugarcane with molasses, vanilla, and spice. It is an unbelievable rum that will make your Havana Club dreams come true.

OTHER SPIRITS, CORDIALS, LIQUEURS, AND APERITIFS

AGWA DE BOLIVIA COCA LEAF LIQUEUR: This bright green elixir is made from coca leaf shipped under armed guard from Bolivia to Amsterdam, where it's stripped of the psychoactive cocaine compounds and distilled with thirty-six other botanicals. It has some of the herbaceousness of absinthe, but at only 60 proof (half that of absinthe), it's gently sweet, with an herbal, grassy flavor and a lemony citrus aftertaste.

BARSOL PISCO PRIMERO: This pisco is produced by one of the oldest distillers in Peru. Bodega San Isidro is in the Ica valley at the foot of the Andes mountains, home to very fertile soil and mineral-rich water sources. BarSol is produced from single-varietal Quebranta grapes, which have a unique, aromatic flavor. This pure grape taste really comes through in the spirit, almost like you are biting these grapes fresh off the vine. It is a delicious artisanal spirit that is a standout in any Pisco cocktail.

DIMMI ITALIAN CORDIAL: Dimmi is made from a delicate combination of wheat spirits with a touch of *grappa di Nebbiolo*. The base spirit is infused with a family recipe of herbs and bitters, including licorice, vanilla, rhubarb, ginseng, and bitter orange. It is then infused a second time with peach and apricot blossoms, which adds a distinct aromatic signature. It can be mixed with bold spirits such as mezcal and Bourbon to provide more delicate fruit and floral notes.

DOLIN VERMOUTH: Dolin has been making vermouth in Chambérey since 1879 and is the only AOC for vermouth in France. Dolin uses a combination of up to fifty plants, herbs, and barks in their recipe, and do not add any synthetic flavors. **Dolin Dry** has a bright, clean, herbaceous quality with a crisp, dry finish. **Dolin Rouge** is lighter, slightly dry with just a hint of bitterness, and a fruity sweetness without a cloying, sugary mouthfeel. These vermouths are my go-tos for classic-style cocktails. Both are also great by themselves, served on the rocks with a citrus twist.

ROOT ORGANIC LIQUEUR: In the 1700s, American colonists were introduced to the root tea that Native Americans drank as an herbal remedy. Brewed from sassafras, sarsaparilla, wintergreen birch bark, and other roots and herbs, root tea was used to cure a variety of ailments. The makers of ROOT have tried to replicate the flavors of this tea in this spirit. It is similar in flavor to root beer, but has a bolder digestive quality that stands out in The Roots Beer.

ROTHMAN & WINTER ORCHARD APRICOT LIQUEUR: Rothman & Winter Orchard apricot liqueur combines juice from the seasonal harvest of Austria's famed Klosterneuburger apricots (known locally as "Marillen") with an eau-de-vie produced from this same fruit. It has a ripe, fresh orchard fruit flavor and bouquet and a long, elegant finish. This is some of the freshest flavors of any cordial I've ever tasted. Use it when you need to add a bright fruit element but don't have any fresh produce on hand.

RESOURCES

BAR SUPPLIES

Amazon.com

BarSupplies.com

Sur La table (www.surlatable.com)

Cocktail Kingdom (www.cocktailkingdom.com): These guys have all the really cool Japanese tools, jiggers, mixing glasses, and other high-end barware.

BITTERS

Atthemeadow.com

FeeBrothers.com

Kegworks.com

Onlybitters.com

scrappysbitters.com

EXOTICS

Lemongrass, shiso leaf, yuzu citrus can be found at Japanese specialty stores.

Dean & DeLuca, Fairway, and select Whole Foods carry edible flowers. Always buy them fresh, never frozen.

PUREES

Borion: This French line of fresh frozen fruit purees can be purchased at www.gourmetfoodstore.com.

SPICES, SALTS, DRIED FRUITS, POWDERS

The Ingredient Finder (www.theingredientfinder.com): Carries elderflower syrup, among other ingredients

Kalustyan's (www.kalustyans.com): Amazing Indian spice shop in New York that has all sorts of spices, dried fruits, and dried chilies.

La Boite Biscuits and Spices (www.laboiteny.com): This shop has all types of exotic spices and powders like smoked cinnamon.

My Spice Sage (www.myspicesage.com): Hickory smoked salt and Kaffir lime powder can be ordered here.

TEAS

Rare Tea Cellar (www.rareteacellar.com)

Spices and Tease (www.spicesandtease.com)

ACKNOWLEDGMENTS

HOW IN THE HELL DID THIS BOOK GET WRITTEN ANY WAY?

Let's start were it all began: thanks to my family for creating such an amazing playground of garden ingredients for a child to grow up with. And special thanks to my grandmother, Oma, for leaving that big jug of Burgundy lying around.

I owe a lot to the amazing chefs I've worked with over the years: Eric Ripert, Jean-Georges Vongerichten, and Jeffery Zakarian. These guys elevated my palate and reshaped how I construct and balance flavors in my recipes.

Thanks to my second family of chefs, true friends that I have eaten, drank, and cooked with over the years: Mike Carmona, Soa Davies, Matt Boudreau, Mark Spitzer. They have been an ongoing source of inspiration for my culinary creativity. A big shout out to my ultimate drink-tasting guinea pig and personal psychiatrist Jeremie Kittredge, for all the fortune-cookie wisdom regarding business and personal matters. And thank you Joanna Wasick for making me a better and more punctual man.

To my partners at the Summit Bar, Hamid and Dimitri, who provided me with my first platform to showcase all these damn tasty cocktails, and a big reason I have the opportunity to write this book.

Thank you to my agent Laura Nolan for helping me get this deal finalized. My editor Caitlin Leffel, who I tortured with many personal delays but she still worked her magic and got my ass to finish the book with the help of ever expanding deadlines. Francis Harris swooped in to help save the day in the later stages and managed to translate the chaos in my brain to organized thoughts on paper. Thanks to Rosanne Kang for some very insightful design advice. My photographer Noah Fecks was a true wizard with the camera. And a special thank you to Jim Meehan for his kind words in the front of the book.

Special thanks to Crystal Classics, Fortessa, Riedel, and Steelite for all their beautiful glassware.

And here's to my crew of bartenders I have shaken, drank, and traveled with over the years: Brian Miller, Joaquin Simo, Dushan Zaric, Eben Freeman, Gardner Dunn, Trevor Schneider, Mark Rancourt, Gary Regan, Jacob Briars, Perry Cornelius, Daniel Undhammer, and the rest of you guys and girls.

Finally, thanks to all the customers and friends in the industry that support our business of liquid happiness.

Here's to sharing a drink on the same side of the stick —SEIDER

INDEX

GREG SEIDER has worked at notable culinary and cocktail destinations such as The Mercer Kitchen, Asia de Cuba, The Box, Minetta Tavern, and The Standard Hotel in Miami. In 2009, he opened The Summit Bar, which *New York Magazine* named Best New Cocktail Bar that year. He created the cocktail program for the lounge at the three Michelin-starred restaurant Le Bernardin and co-owns the restaurants Prima and Manhattan Cricket Club.

NOAH FECKS is a photographer, photography teacher, and the author of the blog and book *The Way We Ate: 100 Chefs Celebrate a Century at the American Table.*

JIM MEEHAN worked at some of New York City's most popular restaurants and bars, including Gramercy Tavern and the Pegu Club, before opening PDT with Brian Shebairo in 2007. Meehan is the Deputy Editor of *Food & Wine*'s annual cocktail book and is the author of *The PDT Cocktail Book.*

First published in the United States in 2014
by Rizzoli International Publications, Inc.
300 Park Avenue South
New York, NY 10010
www.rizzoliusa.com

ISBN: 978-0-8478-4218-6
Library of Congress Number: 2013952716

2014 2015 2016 2017
10 9 8 7 6 5 4 3 2 1

Design by Jan Derevjanik

Photographs by Noah Fecks

Cover illustration by Alex Ostroy

Printed in China